On the Edge of Greatness

A Real Conversation on How Black Women Can Take

Over by Powerfully Running for Office

~

A book by: Tonya Burke

Foreword by: Kimberly Ellis

May you have the faith of a mustard seed that will elevate you to move mountains.

2019

~DEDICATION~

To My Quad Squad – The loves of my life:
My heavenly Father Jesus Christ
My "down for whatever" husband Jason
My "DNA cheerleading children" Devon, Brianna, & Jaylyn
My "fight the power" parents, Herbert & Corine

You each have encouraged me to defy every odd that has attempted to hinder me.

Table of Contents

~Acknowledgments~

To my Chin Checking Crew: Linda, Alexis, Valtina, Yvonne, Flo, James, Ricardo, Alan, Darren, Alisha, Blanca, Tiffany, Rev. Ealy, Betty, and Maxine. I thank each of you for your prayers, guidance and support.

To Kimberly Ellis, I thank you. Your compassion and love for the good in politics will never go unrecognized. Continue to fight the good fight and know that you are surrounded in love.

To Tesa Colvin, who helped me take several years of me procrastinating in writing this book and miraculously getting me to write it in four hours poolside while sipping on a glass of wine. You truly are the "Book Whisperer."

To all my sisters, past and present, that have been told that you are "TOO *(fill in the blank)*," know that you are the decedents of greatness and royalty. The next time someone utters any words of defeat against your life, give them the coldest side-eye because you belong to a Sisterhood of Highly Innovative Trailblazers – WE ARE THE S.H.I.T.!

From whom the whole body, joined and held together by every joint with which it is equipped, when each part is working properly, makes the body grow so that it builds itself up in love. - Ephesians 4:16

1

I know what it is to be in need, and I know what it is to have plenty. I have learned the secret of being content in any and every situation, whether well fed or hungry, whether living in plenty or in want. I can do all this through him who gives me strength. — Philippians 4:12-13

Do not be anxious about anything, but in everything by prayer and supplication with thanksgiving, let your requests be made known to God. And the peace of God, which surpasses all understanding, will guard your hearts and your minds in Christ Jesus. Philippians 4:6-7 ESV

LET'S DO THIS!

Foreword

Hugely gregarious, humble, and gracious in spirit, Tonya Burke is a political dynamo who has written a must-read manual for Black women who dream of running for office. A former elected official herself, Tonya spent nearly five years in the "belly of the beast," brilliantly navigating the potholes, roadblocks, set-ups, and setbacks of running for and serving in elected office while B&F: Black and Female.

This easy to read page-turner pulls back the proverbial curtain and exposes, in a very real and raw way, the realities of a broken - and oftentimes corrupt - political system that is designed to keep women out (and especially Black women!) at all costs.

But in order to play and win the game, you gotta know the game, and this is where On the Edge of Greatness comes in. Tonya has provided a roadmap, chock-full of personal anecdotes, to help Black women understand the political process and how to find the skills and the courage to insert ourselves in.

The indomitable Congresswoman Shirley Chisholm said it best, "If they don't give you a seat at the table, bring a folding chair."[i] On the Edge of Greatness is Tonya Burke's rallying call for Black women to stand up - with no excuses and no apologies - let our voices be heard, pull up a folding chair, and take our rightful seat at the decision-making table.
Run, don't walk, to get your copy today!

Kimberly Ellis
Former Executive Director of Emerge California
Former Candidate for Chair of the California Democratic Party

INTRODUCTION

SORRY NOT SORRY
YOUR OFFICIAL WARNING LABEL

"We don't need Black faces that don't want to be a Black voice," [ii]– Ayanna Pressley

Let me start off by saying that I am Christian, I am Black, and I am Woman. Throughout these pages, I will make reference to each and every one of these areas of identification because they are the bedrock of how I live my life. If you are opposed to me referring to any one of these areas as we dig deep in this word, I give you permission to close the book, not go any further, and go on about your merry life. Please know and understand that I AM NOT willing to censor my story, compromise my views or integrity, alter my ego, devalue my values, disregard my belief system, support what I don't want to support, cut off my blessings, dull my light, remove myself out of the equation, dance to the wrong beat, play to the incorrect sheet of music, or be silent in order to advance the agenda or raise the esteem of anyone else, including those of you who may be consuming this text. You need to know and understand that this will be a take it or leave it journey, and it ain't for the faint at heart. I will speak truth, life, light, and prosperity, whether it feels pleasant to you, stings like hell, or it downright hurts. I am going to say what many of my colleagues in this political game wish they could but are too damn afraid to say.

4

Secondly, let me also say that I am a CUSS-ER and am country as hell (straight from Carson, CA, and never lived in the south). Yes, I said I cuss, and a whole hell of a lot and will make up a word that isn't grammatically correct in a minute. No, I am not proud of it. Nor do I wear it like a badge of honor, but it is what I do. It is an excitable and passionate form of expression that I use. Deacon Jones and Sister Johnson, before you are ready to cast that stone and judge me, pray for me and give me an opportunity. Look'ee here! Growing up, I had a mother that was a serial cusser. She cussed morning, noon, and night. Hell, she even cussed in her damn sleep. She regularly cussed like a sailor, and I am not referring to Popeye. When I came out of her womb, she probably was cussing. Naturally, we sometimes take on the characteristics of our parents, and I am guessing she handed that cussing gene right on down to me. The saying "I get it from my momma" rings true in this case. Even though for many decades, I have served as the official Director of the cussing ministry, I am really working on changing my potty mouth behavior and in rehab for my cussing ailment. You will be happy to know that I have demoted myself from the Director to a general member, so don't even try to judge me. In making an effort of improvement, I did my doggone best to not curse TOO MUCH throughout this book. Just understand that I couldn't go full cold turkey, so I must warn you that there are a few times in this book where my passion got the best of me, I did slip out a few expletives and there will be many moments where I break all of the grammatical rules you may have learned in grade school. So, bottom line, if you have a problem with my cussing, feel free to take it up with my momma. If you know my momma like I know my momma, you could quickly learn that you're better off taking two seats and bearing with the cussing. If you are one of those anal folks and are a member of the grammar police team, and have a problem with my grammar, please feel free to use your red ink pen and mark up this book with corrections as you so choose.

Now that we got the housekeeping formalities out of the way, ladies, we are going to just jump right on into this. I know that you all are used to reading those books that first hold your hand, then take you to the bosom, and end by gently stroking your head into you achieving your greatness. No, ma'am! We're not doing that today! *On the Edge of Greatness: A Real Conversation on How Black Women Can Take Over by Powerfully Running for Office*, just isn't one of those types of books. We aren't going to sit around a bonfire, roast marshmallows, and sing folk songs. We are getting into the nitty-gritty of why you should be leading and running this world and putting you up on the game that is needed to strategically play, in order to make sure that you do it successfully.

I am not here to judge you. I'm here to ACTIVATE you. If you are looking for me to help you passively fit into a system and a world that has never had any real intentions on you thriving in it and be successful, take two seats. I am here to push and promote you to be a disruptor and turn the status quo upside freaking down. If you are interested in politics, leadership, public service, or just have a desire to change the freaking world (okay at least a neighborhood); you are in the right freaking place. If you want to be of service to others for their betterment, and being the total BADASS (Bold Acclaimed Daring Ambitious Savvy Sistah) that you were born to be while doing it, this book is definitely for you. Bluntly speaking, this book is not intended for those women who are resource hoggers wanting only to uplift themselves and their personal selfish agendas, but those that have a great interest in uplifting and furthering the advancement of the Black community (all ethnicities and cultures welcomed). This book right here is not one of those sappy, springtime, and flowery approaches to getting you to run for public office or claiming your spot in leadership. This isn't one of those technical and dry political books riddled with stats and instructions on how to run a decent campaign. This book does what many published political campaign books, training programs, strategists, consultants, and coaches don't and won't do, and that is - provide a real conversation and a call to action with the aim of building Black women's strength and confidence to take on political leadership roles. If you are looking for the words within these pages to coddle you, to get you to embrace your femininity carefully, then I highly suggest that you close the damn book, cut off the audio, or click out of your device. There are far too many other books out there that will do that for you. So, why

6

in great tarnation would I need to duplicate what's already out there. I will not spend any time reinforcing that victim girly girl bullshit that you have been taught all your lives or that trendy misogynistic "think like a man and act like a woman" perspective that mostly insecure men have been pushing on you. "Hell to the naw!" I wrote this book to get you fired up like you've never been fired up before; for you to recognize that you are already freaking great, and for you to understand that you have everything that is needed for you to go out there and rightfully claim your seat on the throne of politics and leadership. My goal is to not only invigorate you but also piss you off to the point that you just get up off the damn couch and run to the clerk's office to file your papers and start your campaign; for you to make a decision to work on a BADASS Black woman's campaign; or pull out your checkbook, debit, or credit card to fund a BADASS Black woman's campaign. I am here to fill in the gaps that many other books have left out by preparing you and providing you with the armor that you will need to fight, what will probably be one of the most treacherous battles that you may ever fight in your life and figuring out your BADASS quotient that will allow you to obtain and succeed in leadership. We are going to talk and address the issues that have hurt like a B-12 shot, but we will not stand in that hurt. We will address, recognize, and move forward to better operate in a hurtful world for our benefit. I am going to be candid with each and every one of you because from this point forward we are girlfriends, kicking it in my living room on a late afternoon, having a deep and meaningful conversation over a glass of perfectly chilled Moscato (oh yes, that is my drink of choice). So, kick back on my big brown plushy couch, put your feet up on the downy ottoman (Not on my couch. We aren't having an Eddie Murphy and Rick James moment today), and take unlimited sips of wine, water, or whatever your beverage of choice; as we take a deep dive into this long-overdue conversation we are about to have together. Oh, no, you didn't just say that you are hungry too. Well, I'm going to tell you just like I tell all my other girlfriends I supply the wine, you "bring your own damn snacks."

Chapter 1 - Hell to the Naw

Black women have had to develop a larger vision of our society than perhaps any other group. They have had to understand white men, white women, and black men. And they have had to understand themselves. When black women win victories, it is a boost for virtually every segment of society. ~Angela Davis

Ok, we're just going to take a nosedive right off the diving board into the deep end. Did I mention that I don't even know how to swim? Here we go: YES, the freaking political parties ain't about S.H.I.T. Now, before any of you get your undies gathered in an unnatural and unflattering wad, lend me a moment to present my point. For the past three, four years or so, us Black women have pulled together and increased our organized efforts by making various pleas to the political powers that be humbly and nicely requesting for increased support for Black elected leaders, candidates, and causes. Some of these politicos have decided to answer our pleas with superficial luncheons, tea parties, BBQs, fish fry's and lame-ass social media apologies that are about as empty as the ones given by Ike Turner's character in "*What's Loves Got To Do With It.*" I am about to say something that would typically get you banished and cast out of some of the greatest political circles. You don't have to worry, because I will take this one for the team. Both the Democratic and Republican parties have proven to be dismissive of black women, consistently overlooking our greatness. Remember how the Democratic party fell out against Congresswoman Maxine Waters like a kid throwing a "You took my lollipop," tantrum when she decided to call out President

Trump and his inhumane shenanigans, as well as her push for what many in the US would classify as a justifiable impeachment. Now they are all fighting to jockey for credit for leading the attempted efforts in Oval Office eviction of Trump. For many decades, the Democratic party has used the Black woman's organizing and voting power to get their choice candidate into office. For example, black women showed up, showed out, and were the primary factor in Senator Doug Jones becoming the elected choice in Alabama. As I excitedly watched so many Black women run shop during that election for the life of me, I couldn't understand and frequently asked myself why the hell didn't those Black women just run a great sister for the seat? My guess is we fell for what I call the "great white hype" theory. We traded the cow for the five magic beans in believing the myth that black women aren't electable and especially in heavily contested political seats. One would think we are witnessing a repeat in this upcoming presidential election with the Black women's overwhelming support and backing of Joe Biden.

The Republican party y'all ain't off the hook either. R-pubs only appear to have love for us when they are having that "See, I have one black friend" or "Look at my African American" conversation. One would think that Mia Love, Omarosa, Candace Owens, and Stacy Dash (pray for this shattered esteem child as she now publicly claims to be White) are the last four lonely Black women that are members of the Republican Party and even they have received a public edge snatching from the members of their own tribe.

The reality is no political party will ever fully commit to us, as long as we continue to allow them only to entertain and be with us during late nights, behind closed doors, just as long as we are footing the bill, or we continue to serve as their metaphorical booty call, making every positive and even negative effort to run and save them during their cries of distress. Black women, we have gotten so entrenched in our love and dedication for our political parties that we have frequently neglected to include the wellbeing of ourselves into our own equation. Our infatuation of belongingness and acceptance has blinded us from the perpetual abuse received from the political parties. We have been programmed within a lifetime of political bullying and vote guilt-tripping into accepting what should be unacceptable to us. We have been long sufferers of Stockholm Syndrome.

Black women, we have proven that we are a formidable Sisterhood of Highly Innovative Trailblazers (the S.H.I.T. I was referring to earlier) worthy of the highest consideration and support politically. All political parties, on all levels (national, state, local) have proven time and time again that they ain't about us. "If politics was a living and breathing human being, black women would be its brain, its heart, and soul – its lifeline." It is us Black women who have demonstrated throughout decades that we are a force in all landscapes of politics – in the field, the campaign offices, on the dais, and financially. Yes, I do appreciate the fact that more political parties and a few presidential candidates are riding on a new wave and have hired on more dynamic Black women to lead in the party (We see you Muthoni Wambu Kraal and Symone D. Sanders) and serve on their campaigns. Please do understand that these changes happened as the direct result of Black women pushing back, organizing and demanding a seat at the table. Please don't allow yourselves to fall for the Chameleon Effect and thinking that we have made it, and we can now sit back and relax. We must continue to hold the folks making these decisions to the line and accountable.

I decided to write and dedicate this book for and to Black women across the globe. My Sisters! I must preface the fact that I am not specifically referring to the widely popular notion of "woman of color" because the issues and needs of the Black woman tend to frequently get lost in the translation, only to end up being diluted with the usage of the term. "Woman of color" is, in my opinion, a "politically correct" term and "Mary Poppins" way that this country has scapegoated addressing the plight and devastation of the Black woman. Generally speaking, the United States loves to take a half-ass approach at helping one specific ethnic group, by lumping all the ethnic and cultural groups together and implying that we all have the same issues, needs, and concerns. What has happened is we have a government that has completely failed at fully addressing any of the issues of any of the women that identify with any of the ethnic and cultural groups. "American public politics and policies has caused the weaponization of black women," which has been purely based on the colors of our skin (Yes, we do come in all shades). As a result, we regularly are exposed to discrimination, bias, violence, oppression, and poverty. The overall thought is not only Black but all "women of color" are expected to adapt to the country's ideals of the norm, which currently is and has always been the Caucasian man and woman.

Don't get me wrong! Yes, there are a shortage women across all ethnicities serving in public office (Asian, Pacific Islander, Latino, Caucasian, Native American, etc.), but this book serves as an anthem, a love letter, a manifesto to my sisters whose roots originate from the African Diaspora. No matter if your ancestral long charted destiny has landed you in Asia, Europe, Australia, the Caribbean, Africa, or on freaking Plymouth Rock, I am speaking volumes to YOU, my sisters. My Black people, we need to stop getting caught up in those asinine debates about whether or not you are more Black or worthy because you were born in the United States. No matter where we are around this globe, Black women have been and continue to be oppressed. Can this book be beneficial for women of other races and cultures? Of course, it can. Any woman of any race and culture can read through the pages of this book and be deeply enriched and experience positive changes in their lives or feel compelled to help improve the lives of others. I do suggest that any and everyone read this book. One thing that I have learned in my forty plus years on this planet called Earth, is that women of other races can't adequately support, ride or die for, or march in the streets on behalf of Black women if they truly have not taken the time to learn enough about our strengths, our shortcomings, what makes us the special beings that we are. Non-Black women who long to rally on our behalf should desire to be so tight with us, that if for example we get discriminated against and get fired from a job due to our natural hairstyles (grateful for the recent protections put in place by recent legislature in California- big ups to champion and Political Badass and Senator Holly Mitchell, as well as in New York.), they in turn get enraged and concerned as if they themselves got fired from the job. Hell, some of them might even feel compelled to go out and get a natural hairstyle. Never mind, we don't need another Rachel

Dolezal fallout. Black women don't need any more bandwagon, fair-weather friends who don't want to put in the work. Those that are only riding along for national credit and fulfilling their own personal gain. If that is your agenda, please keep those fraudulent "we shall overcome" I'm ready to make myself feel good like I have really done something moments to yourself. I'm speaking of those non-Black chicks that will use you and your community clout to put a march together, have you rally up and excite all the folks for the cause, but as soon as the day ends and the cameras disappear, so do their support. My sisters, this is where we go wrong. We settle for the short-term euphoric feel good, instead of DEMANDING that the short term becomes our way of life. Our new freaking normal. Uh oh! I used the wrong damn 'D' word. People in politics tend to want to scurry away from including demands in any of their dialogue when it comes to the improvement in the conditions of Black folks. When Black folks start demanding, they get labeled as militant. Folks in politics seem to feel that it's not in comparison to the other popular and overly used 'D' word – Democracy, which in my eyes is what we as Black women have been asking for.

I also don't have any beef with any of the fellas out there, especially given that I lie down, go to sleep and wake up next to a fine ass Black brother every night and day. There are intricate roles that our male counterparts can play in supporting Black women, which we welcome and will further discuss a tad bit later.

So, someone may still be asking why write a book focusing on Black women and political leadership? If you have to ask that question, we have more work to do than I thought.

WHY THE HELL NOT! I don't need to spew off a bunch of convoluted statistics for you all to know that there are far, few and in between when it comes to the number of black women being supported, running for, winning, and serving public office on a national, state, and local level. I am also speaking of those often hidden and secret appointments that exist on every level, leadership in the political parties, political staffers, campaign operatives, and the list goes on and on. Black women are diminishing in these positions like an endangered species but without the pleasure of being granted a protected classification.

Just in case you were thinking it, NO, it didn't take the electing of Donald Trump, a president that emulates the awful stench of white supremacy, for me to come to the realization of the importance of this subject matter and therefore drove me to put pen to paper. In the voice of the late and great Whitney Houston, "Hell to the naw!"
Just in case you were thinking it, NO, it didn't take the election of Barak Obama, the first Black man to be elected as President of the United States, for me to have a feel-good moment and a sudden epiphany of the state of Black women in politics thus leading me to put pen to paper. Hell to the naw!

Just in case you are thinking it, NO, it didn't take former Secretary of State Hillary Clinton running and not succeeding on two different occasions for the bid of the President of the United States for me to have an "I am every woman" moment and put pen to paper. Hell to the naw!

Nor did it take Oprah Winfrey (even though I am a huge fan) giving one of what many felt was the most moving speeches on the sexual assault #MeToo movement, causing just about every woman around the country to get excited about the possibility of them having the rare opportunity of voting the 'O' in as the first Black woman President of the United States. Hell, to the naw!

Between you and me, I love Oprah and would vote for her tomorrow if given the opportunity.
Here is the real deal. I've been a Black woman living in the United States for over 40 years and the oppression of Black women has been in existence long before 46-1 had the opportunity to coin the slogan "you're fired," didn't disappear with the presence of a Black man serving in the highest position on US soil, didn't lighten up since the presidential election run of a woman, or hasn't de-escalated since the queen of daytime talk graced us with her

13

empathic words. Please don't get all bedazzled by the hype, because folks out here all of a sudden having an epiphany and have served up a temporary #WOKE moment about racism and sexism. That shit has been the bedrock of the Black woman's oppression from the moment that they strapped us onto the slave ships, or what Kanye and Kim Kardashian West would probably refer to as cruise liners.

Honestly, I wrote this book as the result of me being sick and tired of being sick and tired of seeing far too many BADASS Black women not serving in public office and leadership roles, them being hesitant and feeling the need to get permission to seek leadership in public office for a multitude of self-defeating reasons, and many of them being told that they aren't or weren't "the one." It took me seeing far too many BADASS Black women being dissed, dismissed, and disrespected by the political parties they have been so dedicated to serving; and having to beg, borrow and steal to so much as get any form of political support. If you have done any research on me, you would have learned that I am a registered Democrat. But, please don't think for one damn moment that I am favoring one party over the other when it comes to the security of Black women. All the parties have displayed minimal if any sense of honor or loyalty to Black women, the fiercest and most dedicated voting bloc in the nation. So, I figured why continue to take my complaints about it to Facebook or on the poor soul trying to eat in the lunchroom at work. How about I step up and do something about it? Wala! There you have it. Also, I have some skin in this political game, as I have personally served as a Black female politician, am a political candidate development coach, and a political strategist that has had the opportunity to work with all types of political candidates and campaigns; So, I have walked the walk and have earned my spot to talk the talk. I have seen firsthand how politics has reared its ugly racist and sexist head towards Black women. Black women have a systematic, purpose-driven, and unfair disadvantage in this political game. I have personally seen the existence of this deeply rooted plan unfolding and put into action. Just about every time I walk into a political place and space or take a seat at a political table, I don't see enough women that look like me. Yes, "THEY," say a record number of women, including Black women, ran for public office in 2018. Yes, some of these women won their races. Let me digress and have one of my ADHD moments because I realize that I have unconsciously fallen into the "THEY" zone. You know how us Black folks do with THEY. Every time we have a conversation mentioning others, we refer to "THEY" as if it is some secret society group or like the group of white folks in the movie "Get Out," which congregated and conspired to harvest Black men's bodies. Well, in this case, "THEY" refers to just about every media source on the planet. I remember spending much of 2018 reading article after article, social media post after social media post each showcasing a woman or group of women that decided to dust off their fears, pride, egos, or whatever else that had been holding them back, to make the mad dash to run in the election of their choosing.

We saw various political journalists egging us on to watch out for specific women who were running. Many of these stories included women that we probably didn't personally know or any of those Black women that were running within our own communities. According to BlackWomenInPolitics.com 468 black women ran for office in 2018: 58 for federal seats, 180 for state seats, 213 for local seats and 17 not specified, 178 in blue states, 290 in red states, 181 incumbents, and 287 challengers. 6 black women ran as Republicans for congress. We witnessed Stacy Abrams, a fierce and humble Black woman run for the Governor of Georgia being coined as one of the most dynamic candidates and political BADASSES to run in any race this past 2018 (my opinion she actually won the election, but that is commentary for another book). Abrams stayed true to her roots (literally that natural doo was fierce!) and at no time code-switching to fit in with mainstream society's political correctness. She reached out to the often-forgotten areas of rural Georgia and voters that no one dared to reach out to, all while fighting the good fight against voter suppression. She was politically astute and experienced well before the race and had a proven track record dating back to her high school and college years. We have seen since that race these same media platforms jumping on the who should run for president or vice president in 2020 bandwagon. Initially, Abrams was not even granted a soft mention as a formidable candidate on a presidential/vice presidential ticket for the upcoming 2020 election. All while other white and wannabe candidates were getting simultaneous thumbs up and nationwide nods. You do the doggone math. Lemme just say this right here, if Stacey Abrams threw her hat in the ring and decided to run for president in 2020 or any other year, I would send her all of my coins, cavass all day and all night, and cast my vote for her.

Just in case any of you have forgotten. There were times in history when African women were queens and ruled nations. And that was the norm. [iii]You're here reading this book because you know it's time to return to claim your legacy and stomp out this roach-infested way of life imposed by the hateful. We must begin to declare that we will no longer be drinking the poisoned Kool-Aid and turning around and serving it to the other queens in our tribe.

It's time out for the talking. The next step is to get your ass in gear, take action, and make it happen. (Lockhart, 2018)

Chapter 2 - If Serving Is Beneath You, Then Leading Is Beyond You

"There is always something to do. There are hungry people to feed, naked people to clothe, sick people to comfort, and make well. And while I don't expect you to save the world I do think it's not asking too much for you to love those with whom you sleep, share the happiness of those whom you call friend, engage those among you who are visionary and remove from your life those who offer you depression, despair, and disrespect." – Nikki Giovanni

I am so excited! Gurl, you just don't know how excited I am to know that you are even taking me boldly pushing you into politics into consideration. You and I know that it is so difficult for us, as Black women, to be able to break into this field. But I'm so happy that you have decided in some capacity to do so. WE all need you. This world needs you. Your community needs you. Our schools need you, um, the people in the damn bank, the people at the mall, the people at the grocery store, the people at the gas station, don't act like you ain't knowing. You play such an important role in the evolution of this world. You play such an important role in making sure that this world is a better place. It's a choice. Not everybody makes that choice and for a multitude of reasons. Some people don't do it because they, you know, they never step into their purpose because of fear. Black women have been the untitled leaders and the hidden gems of this world from the beginning of our existence. It is us that has taken every man, woman, and child to our bosoms (literally) and cared for and nurtured them. It is us that has been the secret backbone of just about every meaningful movement that has taken place around the world.

I know that many of you are thinking, well, I've never been a leader. My response will more than likely be "yes, you have." I get that all the time. I recently met a young woman, and she expressed her desire to enter politics. She indicated that she was thinking about running for school board, but it has been a real struggle for her because she keeps telling herself, "I've never been a leader." I don't think that I've ever met a person in life that has never led that hasn't served in some form of leadership capacity. Now I didn't say that they all lead well, but everyone has led. Like this woman, we often develop these unwritten rules or criteria of what a leader should be. Often times throughout life we have been through so much hurt and unrepaired damage that there is no way in hell we will ever place the characteristics that make us the S.H.I.T. on that list. We will box ourselves into an equation that doesn't add up to us leading. One of the issues is that, what you have envisioned your entire life as a leader, is not who you see in the mirror or anyone that closely resembles that. If we can adjust some of that stinkin thinkin, we will be all good.

My curiosity was sparked with this young woman, as it always is when women express any desire to get into politics. I dug a little deeper beyond her superficial and safe zone surface, asking questions about her and her life. Upon her telling me her accomplishments, she just played each experience off as nothing special and just a way of life. I was like, "Damn! You are just like me; you've been leading since you were school age." I, too, discredited my leadership ability and capacity when I was asked to run for office. Like many of us, I discarded those worthwhile experiences too. I didn't fully realize that I had truly been selling myself short until I decided to run for city council. When I was contemplating on running, I reached out to my parents, because I wanted to get the blessings of my family. You know, you kind of want to vet things with your family or those who truly love, care, and appreciate you. In some instances, that may not be your family. My family serves as my rock. These are the people who I love dearly, and they exert the same level of love towards me. So, it meant a lot to me to get their support.

I remember sharing my political decision with my parents and my dad saying, "We were wondering what took you so long." He said, "your mother and I always spoke about how you would grow up to either be an attorney or a politician." That totally blew me away, because I realized that my parents saw in me at an early age, what I wasn't even able to see in myself as a grown woman. After a few minutes into the conversation, I thought to myself, "Wait a damn minute! y'all thought I was going to be an attorney or a politician. Hell, those are the two professions that people always criticize, ridicule, or are called crooks and criminals." For a brief moment, I gave my parents one of those cold Black girl side-eyes, and then my parents redeemed themselves when they stated that they have always witnessed my heart go out to and my desire for what's best for the people. They noticed that in just about every area of my childhood and adult life, I have spent time serving others. See, my parents taught me at an early age that my purpose in life is to serve God and to serve God's people. So, I have always had that ingrained in me my entire life. But I didn't make that connection to being a good leader until I answered my political calling.

See, I started my business Hidden Gems Enterprise, because I want to start not only a movement but a new way of life for Black women across the globe. I want to help those dynamic women that have been making groundbreaking behind the scenes moves within agencies, businesses, and their communities, be able to obtain leadership positions in the areas of their choosing. Not just in politics, we need to also be in corporate boardrooms. We need incredible Black women seated at all tables.

There are some of you (you know who you are) that won't do a damn thing to help anyone, because you don't give two shitakes about anyone else. You are strictly in it for yourself. Yeah, I just called your selfish ass out. Point blank period. But it is my hope and my desire that the majority of you out there are wanting to be that change agent. You are that thought leader that said, "I want to be the change that I want to see happen." You want to be the catalyst in improving this world. I'm pretty sure you're watching the same bullshit that I'm watching on a daily in the news and seeing all the unnecessary political posturing that is causing devastation around the world. I know you see all the loss of life. We're seeing so many Black men and women being shot down and killed at the hands of those that took an oath to protect and serve. Let me go further and add that not all serving in law enforcement are heinous killers. There are a few Klan thought infested individuals that have made their way into the circle of blue. There are always some bad apples in the bunch, and lately, we see so many of those bad apples that it's making the whole orchard appear to be rotten. We're seeing our young folks not receiving the education that they need. We're seeing racism and hatred come out of dormancy, where Black folks are having law enforcement called out on them for just engaging in activities of daily living

#WateringTheGrassWhileBlack Let's not fool ourselves. Racism has been woven through the threads of the thirteen stripes and fifty stars, and there are those who will always be hell-bent on it, always being the principal fabric of the good ole red, white, and blue. It has been very surprising for many, but not for those of us that truly know the foundation and history of this country; that we've seen a heightened level of activity that's happening across the nation where people are purpose-driven towards inciting hate and are diligently recruiting other fools into their cause. This is why it's so important that if serving in public office is what you truly want to do, you're doing so because you're a true servant leader. You're a compassionate leader. You're a leader that wants to serve people and not-self. Let me just tell you right now, if your intention is to get into politics because you want to be rich, powerful, famous, or you want everybody to follow behind you, then you and your narcissistic ass need to go somewhere else. You need to try something different because this isn't, or least, this shouldn't be the field for you. Yeah, you may gain some power, no matter the position or capacity in which you serve. You may even build a following, a fan club, or a local political base of voters, residents, students, teachers, etc.

You may even have an opportunity to serve on a leadership platform where your name stays in the news, and you gain a sense of unwanted popularity. A clear example of a Political Badass and dynamic woman in politics that regularly receives media attention regardless if the coverage is shown in a positive or negative light is Congresswoman

Maxine Waters. Congresswoman Waters has served in politics for many years. She has always served her communities. Hell, she has been coined as "everyone's Congresswoman." In the last few years her visibility has increased in all forms of media due to her bold and daring stance to speak out against what she feels is wrong. In personally knowing Congresswoman Waters, I can bet $25 that she is and has not spoken out, for the sole purpose that she has a desire to be famous. In all honesty, I believe that she could give a shit if you called her "Auntie Maxine." What she wants you to do is get off your derriere and help her in this fight. I'm pretty sure she would like for you to also feel moved and compelled to get out there and write her a donation check for her campaign, walk and knock on some doors, have her back on a physical and mental level, so that she can continue to serve the people in the capacity that she has been able to serve OR greater. Waters and a few other notable politicians are unapologetic Black women that do not care what anybody says or thinks about them and will still get out there and do the work.

When you are a servant leader, when you are a compassionate leader, when your sole focus is to work on behalf of the people, you are going to get beat up metaphorically. Many of the Black women including myself who have served politically, have suffered unwarranted attacks. We do what is needed for us to step out there and get on the frontline unapologetically, unapologetically call out the bull shitake (no I'm not referring to mushrooms. I told you that I'm trying not to cuss), and unapologetically lead by no means necessary. If you are going into this thinking that everyone will love you, hell, even like you, No ma'am! No, ma'am! No, ma'am! DO NOT pass 'Go' and DO NOT collect $200. I warned you that we were going to have a real conversation with no sugar sprinkled on top. You may not be popular amongst those that want to do harm. Frack them and their bull shitake! Nor should you strive to make that your goal. Your primary and unabated focus is to serve the PEOPLE. There are some mean and evil folks out there, and some of them are sitting in these seats with titles like President, Congressman, Senator, Mayor, School Board Trustee, just to name a few. Contrary to the twisted messages that some fools out there are attempting to push to black women; we do have the power to move these folks the hell out of the seats and get them the hell out of our way so that we can progress and get the real business done. The changes that you will make in the lives of the folks that you are going to serve will surpass all of the superficial nonsense. It is important that you hold strong and remain true to those who you serve. It's my belief that when you are fighting the battle against evil, God is going to give you everything that you need to be the victor. God has the ultimate power to protect every hair on your head, every tooth in your mouth, and every cell in your body. Have faith! There is no need to cower down. Yes, I just had a brief preaching moment. Won't He do it! Also know, that when you are on the side of righteousness, your supporters will have your back. Media has a way of only showcasing and putting the focus on the naysayers, which typically are small in numbers. But there are many that will cheer you on and regularly. I have learned that if you are authentic with your constituents and serve them well, they will figuratively slay your enemies for you. Do not be tempted to conform to this unethical nonsense that we have been witnessing in many of our spineless elected leaders. If you rise above, you will have a positive platform, and you will be seen as the dazzling, shining light of hope that you are. You will be noticed for your bold leadership because you're doing something different than this ignorant shit that we are witnessing many of our nations' leaders engaging in right now. You will be in situations where you will have to vote against someone that you love and respect. You just won't have the same viewpoint as they do, and you have to remain true to your constituents. Corporations and individuals will dangle money and/or resources in your face to get you to support something that totally goes against your principles, values, or could be to the detriment of the entity in which you serve. There will be times where you will have to put something that you are yearning to have implemented on the back burner, because of timing, funding, or the simple fact that you can't get support from your colleagues. When that happens, you can't ball up in the corner or throw a temper tantrum and threaten and hold folks livelihoods hostage until you get what you want. That is piss poor leadership that has no business in politics. What I am getting at is don't let the "new" form of politics and leadership that we are observing unfold before our eyes on a daily become your "new normal." That shitake wasn't good over 100 years ago, and that shitake ain't good now, no matter how they try to spin it.

You may not make it in the newspaper, the radio airwaves, or tv, but nothing is more comforting and rewarding than the fact that one of your residents approaches you and says that you made a positive difference in their lives and their family's lives. Hell, that's all the notoriety you need. That was all the "well done" confirmation that I needed to continue to put on my cape (and yes, I have a cape) and fight the good fight on a daily. Just know this, when your platform is based on a good foundation, the good news will spread like chickenpox on a preschool playground. Be bold, be brave, be brilliant, be someone that's different than what you see, and don't like. We don't witness this enough in politics, especially on the local level. Some folks in politics who I have worked with over the years have a lot to say. They have these incredible voices, but they have silenced the voice because they don't want to be viewed in a certain way. They have let the bullies stomp out their fire. When the people you serve are your focus and not the politics, you will be able to withstand all of that. I'm not saying that while you're in office that the only way to show up is not to consider yourself. Not caring for yourself is a road to disaster, and it leads to you suffering from a major burn out. You will end up hating the position, hating the people, and hating what you do. So, hell yeah, you need to take care of you. You need to focus on maintaining good health. You can't serve if you are out of service.

Being a boss and being a leader are two different ways of thinking. If you want to boss others, I'm here to tell you this ain't for you. If you want to lead others, you are in the right place. The slave owner was a boss. Harriet Tubman was a leader. She sacrificed her wellbeing. She sacrificed her life. She sacrificed herself to the point where she could have lost everything because of what she was doing to help free the slaves. That's a leader. It is not about you, and if that is your sole desire, if that is your whole reason for doing this, let me repeat, you ain't the Black woman I'm trying to reach out to. You are not the Black woman who I'm encouraging to run for public office. You are not the Black woman that I'm trying to see as a part of this movement, a part of this crew. I'm just going to be straight up and honest with you, the only thing you need to do is to go sit your ass down. It is what it is. Take it or leave it, and if your primary purpose is you, we do not need you in this capacity. We already have enough of self-indulged, self-fulfilling people in this world that's out there leading. I'm not saying that you don't take care of you in the process because it takes someone who's willing to make positive sacrificial decisions and actions. Someone who's willing to forget about their own personal agendas and who's able to be flexible to do what it is that the people need to be done. So, I'm just saying this shitake ain't about you.

Up until now, it may have been ALL about you. You may have chosen to stay out of the fight that you were destined to fight. You may have chosen to take a passive approach when you shouldn't have, to not rock the boat, or ruffle any feathers. That approached hasn't improved a damn thang for you or those who need you.

So, this is the moment, right now, when you have the opportunity to do something different. Be a disruptor.

How can you show up and lead the way for others WITHOUT getting caught up in what you get out of it or what's easiest for you?

Once you figure out what that is – THEN DO IT!

Chapter 3 - It Takes A Village To Get A Black Woman Into Public Office – Creating Your BADASS Network

The success of every woman should be the inspiration to another. We should raise each other up. Make sure you're very strong, be extremely kind, and above all, be humble. Serena Williams.

In case you weren't aware, just so you know that this process is not intended for you to do it by yourself. You are not meant to go at this alone. The very fact that you are reading this book, you now have access to a new family of black women around the globe that you can lean on for support. You are now a part of the You Tha S.H.I.T. family. And we are so very pleased that you have joined us. It is so important for you to understand and know that far too often as Black women, we are, so very independent. You know, we operate in a way where we don't want anyone to see us operate in our weaknesses. We don't want anyone to see that we experience struggles. So, we do all we can to make sure that we get things done. Sometimes to our detriment. That's just who we are, how we are. So, it's very important for you to know that you don't have to continue to do things within a silo, suffering in silence. It is important for you to develop and create what I call your BADASS network. You know you are a BADASS woman that's going to be doing BADASS things, and it's going to require you to have some BADASS people on your team in order for you to be successful and stay successful.

Quality vs. Quantity

When I ran for city council, I didn't have an extremely large team like many of the other candidates that I ran against. I had just a small group of friends, primarily comprised of women and a "hi-five" number of family members.

I know that some of you have already begun surveying your peeps and feel that you are doomed because you don't know a lot of people. You know, it's just me, my mama or my auntie or you, three of my good homegirls (yes, I said homegirls, because I am a Gen - X'er). Lemme just say that it's okay if you don't have a full platoon because it's not about the quantity. It's about the quality of people that will be working with you. Matter of fact, I consistently had three to five women, who were knocking on the doors, making phone calls, etc., when I ran for office. I didn't need a large group, it would have been nice, but I didn't have one. We were small but mighty. You know, like the crew in the movie 300. My crew had my back at every angle and would whoop and stomp anyone's ass that came incorrect. And they were dedicated. They weren't just dedicated to me, but they were dedicated to the cause, the vision, the mission, and the people.

You can have 300, 400, 500, 600, or more people on your team and only have two people that are worth red beans, rice, and cornbread. The numbers won't make a damn difference if you only have two people who are doing all the work, and you got 98 other shiftless ass people who are just sitting around and taking up space, taking up your time, and energy. That is the last damn thing you need when you are running a campaign or actually serving in office. You want to have a tight network in order to make your life a little bit easier to get it to a point where you can be more productive and are able to serve more people. But if you have to be running around, checking on folks, seeing if they are where they're supposed to be and doing the things that they're supposed to do, that defeats the purpose of them being around in the first place.

A Team That Cares About Your Mission

If you have somebody that's on your team and they are looking down on you, your community and the people in your community as if they are peasants, they're not going to be that beneficial to you because they are going to bring that negative mojo into your camp. A lot of the people in your network are going to serve as your earthly saving grace . These are the ride or dies that will have your back when you go through those times that are very hard. Please mark my words; you're going to go through some times that are really, really, really hard. You're going to have some difficult moments while running for office. There's going to be times, before and during the campaign, and after you get elected; you're just going to be like, I wave the damn white flag; I give this shit up, this just ain't what I signed up for, I can't do it anymore, this is too much for me, and host of other negative thoughts and emotions. I told you we weren't going to bullshit each other. These feelings and experiences are not unusual, so hang in there. This is why it is very pertinent that you have a squad who believes in you, believe in your mission, who believe that you can do the things that you say you can do and will give their right knee to make sure that you achieve your goals. You want supporters who will hold you up when you can't hold yourself up. You don't want to invest your time, energy, and money on those that don't like you, let alone believe in you. You just don't want that cancer to filtrate through your team. This is why, as a political coach and consultant, I make sure that I treat the folks I work with as if I was working on my own campaign, my child's campaign, or my momma's campaign. I give the same attention, love, and care that I would give to myself. With that being said, you have to make sure that you don't turn into Cruella, treating everyone like you own them. You have to be willing to serve as an example for your team. You need to be willing to always put in the work, believe in yourself, the members of your team, the things that you're doing, your vision, and the people who you're going to serve.

Compile Your List of Potential Members

Everyone has the resources to pull off a successful campaign. It just takes some creativity when you are composing your list of supporters to be a part of your BADASS network. There is no magic number of how many should be on your team. Don't focus on how many. Focus on what expertise they have and the talents they will bring to the table. How and what will you learn from them? What expertise do you have that you will be able to bless them with? Remember, this is a two-way transaction. This isn't just a take and continue to take situation; you need to be giving out some of your knowledge, skills, abilities, love, and expertise too. Don't be one of those damn resource hoggers. You know I can't stand those types of folks. Your network should serve as your campaign insulation. I remember when our family purchased and invested in a new home. We had the opportunity of being able to witness each phase of our home being built from the ground up. The time had come in the home building process where we neede to meet with the home design representative and had to make some choices about the interiors of our home. As new and excited homeowners, all we really cared about at that moment was the aesthetics and the stability of the home's structure. We were only focused on what was visible to the naked eye. Throughout this process, the representative kept on sweating us and making a big deal about the type of insulation that we should install into our home. She sweated us so much that I thought that I was going to have to "Snap, Crackle, and Pop" her ass to stop applying so much pressure. At the time, we didn't think much of it and couldn't understand why this woman kept on whining about the insulation and kept on attempting to upsell us on the most expensive insulation they had. I remember telling her that I didn't really care and asked her why in the hell it was a big deal. I just knew that she was going to respond by saying that she was getting some side coins from the manufacturer of the insulation company. This woman damn near fell out of her chair when I asked my question. She said, "the insulation that you install in your home can make a significant difference in whether every summer you have a $600 a month electric bill or in the winter a $400 a month gas bill." Let's just say that she got our attention, and we ended up going with a better-quality insulation, which has saved us significantly. You should look at your BADASS crew the same way. You don't just get what you pay for, but you also get what you invest in. Each member of your BADASS network's goal is to fill in the gaps and to make sure that your political campaign and career are well insulated and prepared for every possible experience. You have to also be invested in yourself and come at least 100%. How can you expect that someone else will give you 100%, and you aren't even delivering 50%? I had a political coaching client that was extremely unresponsive, wanted everyone else to do the work that she was required to do as a candidate, but wanted to spend most of her time worrying about politically insignificant things like logos, theme songs, and slogans (all which I might add, don't win elections). Let's just say that this chick's actions or lack thereof, caused her to lose out on major funding, endorsements, and resources.

Genuine Team Members - Volunteer vs. Hiring

Some of your network members will be friends, some will be family, and some will be people that you have to hire and pay to provide you with a service. That's something that you're going to have to get a grasp on. Everything is not going to be for free, and you can't go around trying to discount everyone's offerings or try to get over on those who you should be paying. Just like you have the expectation that someone, at some point, pays you or provides you with something tangible for the work that you do. If you don't think you are valuable enough to be compensated for your gifts and your talents, we may need to dig deep and do some additional inner work to see where those thoughts of lack stem from. You just can't think, oh, I'm going to get all of these services from this person or all of this help from my team and then don't want to compensate them. Even your volunteers should receive some form of token of your appreciation. Even when I've had friends who have helped me, I have paid or gifted them with something. These folks didn't ask to be paid, they didn't necessarily want to be paid, they provided me a service that someone else would have probably charged me, they did an exceptional job at it, so I felt it was important for me to pay or gift them. Sometimes that meant I provided them with spa days, trips/excursions, etc. The bare minimum that you should be providing your volunteers is a delicious meal. My point here is, don't be stingy and inconsiderate to those that are there to help you out. As the good book says, do unto others as you want them to do unto you. You dog out your network, and you can expect the same in return.

You want good people who aren't just there to collect a check or jock on your new-found public status. In this political industry, there are a number of great people who will go to the edge of a cliff, Thelma and Louise style for you. There are also a bunch of Lucifers out there, preying on their next victim that they will coerce into taking that infamous bite of the forbidden fruit. Like in any other setting, you have to do your due diligence and vet the members of your BADASS NETWORK, whether they are hired or not. Hiring members of your team will oftentime be inevitable, so be prepared to go through a full hiring process. You can even expect to go through a hiring process with your potential volunteers.

Do your homework. Conduct the appropriate research for the race in which you are running. Check out past financial reports to get a sense of what the average rates or fees that the political professional on your team should be paid. These reports are public record and can be obtained from your local city/county clerk, and state/federal political, financial reporting agencies. Also, check with national/state political consultants associations. Don't expect to pay someone the same amount for a small city council race that you would pay for a congressional race. Conduct this research before you hire anyone on to work with you so that you don't get cheated or you don't end up cheating someone.

Know When to Let Someone Go – "You're Fired!"

For the first, second, and the start of my third campaign, I paid a number of individuals to provide a number of different services for me and my campaign. I also had a number of volunteers to help me as well. I've had to discontinue working with a few of both my paid and volunteer team members. For example, I had a terrific consultant. He had a great reputation and record for running great campaigns and winning political elections. As great as the person was, I had to end my contracted services with this individual because he was overextended. His primary job was to be a consultant, so at this time, he took on so many different campaigns that mine was no longer a priority with him and became just a gig. Of course, having another successful campaign on his resume would have been great, but his ultimate goal at the end of the day was to get paid. I get that and totally understand that concept.

So, I had to make the decision, and I had to say, "I'm sorry, but your services are no longer needed." If I hadn't, my campaign probably wouldn't have ended in success, and I probably wouldn't have been elected. Don't get me wrong. There wasn't any love lost. We're still friends to this day. I still call on him and ask questions, and he calls on me and asks questions. There was no ill will, no hard feelings, but he just wasn't for me at that time. So, sometimes, you are going to have those times where someone is just not going to be for you. They may be great for someone else. He's worked on many other campaigns and has been excellent, successful, and worked out just terrific with those folks. But he just wasn't what I needed. He couldn't give me what I needed. So, we had to sever the business relationship. And sometimes that's going to happen with people who you're not even paying people who are volunteers; it happens even with family members. I tell people all the time, if my mama, ain't doing what she's supposed to do; If she's not operating and doing the tasks that she was assigned to do, I'll fire her. I ain't got no problem firing my mama, because the job has to get done. And I know that sounds really, really, really, really, really cruel. But the bottom line is you have a lot of work that you're going to have to do, and you don't have a whole lot of time to do it. You don't need any dead weight on your team.

You Shouldn't Be Every Woman All The Time

When you're running your campaign, that time goes by so fast. You could get started in January, and the next thing you know, you're in July and August, and that's considered go time when it comes to campaigning. I'm going to suggest to you what I always suggest to my clients, start as early as possible. If you are two years out before your election, go ahead and get started in working on your campaign. I have seen candidates that were the shoe in to win had the most money, the favorite of the election, but lost the race due to them not being organized. So, you don't have a whole lot of time to be trying to nurture someone into their position or completing every task in your campaign. You WILL need someone else to help you run your campaign and many of the various intricacies that will be needed in order for you to be successful and win your race. At a minimum, you want to recruit a campaign manager. This person doesn't have to be a paid position. If you are running a very large and expensive race, you will more than likely have to hire a professional campaign manager with political experience and a handle on the campaigning process. You CAN Not (and I repeat) YOU CAN NOT plan your campaign

31

thinking that you will be the one that will be running and doing all of the work. One, because in all honesty, you are the center focus of the campaign and are too involved in the process to make rational decisions. Two, campaigning is a very emotional process, and this can cause you not to use the best judgment, which can cause you to make a decision based on fear, frustration, etc. So, if you are the main person that is handling it all, something is going to fall through the cracks, and you will probably lose your mind in the process. This is a very difficult process for us Type-A folks because we desire to control EVERYTHING. I had this very problem because like I said, I am a very independent person, and I'm a Type-A personality person, I can be very anal, very, you know, "I want it just like this!" I was operating in fear and lack of trust. Operating in the zone of "perfection," I frequently found myself trying to be everything and every woman, and that will NEVER exist. I know that Chaka Kahn and the late great Whitney Houston sang their asses off on both versions of, "I'm every woman," but when it comes to campaigning, you CAN NOT be every damn woman. You have to be the winner. Point Blank Period.

It's okay for you to have every woman on your team, but you don't need to be every woman. Initially, in my campaign, I was delivering the signs, I was the graphic arts designer, the printer, the campaign manager, the consultant, the pastor, and trying to coach myself. You just can't wear all the hats. That's why you have to build a strong network of likeminded people who support you, and it's good to start that process early when you've made this decision to do the damn thing, and I hope that's the decision that you will make after you finish reading this book. I hope your decision is YES. I am going to run for and win public office. I hope your decision at that point is, okay, I'm going to do this now, and I need to start building my network, my BADASS team. Even if you're not going to run for another four or five years, it could be some time away, but you should still initiate building your base, building your team, and your kitchen cabinet; because that's going to be very important.

Allow Yourself to Receive Gifts

I know that some of you are thinking, okay, well, how much is all of this going to cost me? You know, there's no magic number. It may not cost you anything (don't totally count on this). If you have a supportive team of people who have everything that you need that are your friends, family, or colleagues, who want to invest in you by supplying you with their gifts and talents, you may decrease your costs significantly. See, when you're campaigning, giving money isn't the only way that someone can help and support you. You can get what you call in-kind contributions. Contributions aren't just financial. I've had people who have stepped up and said, hey, I'll take care of these postcards for you, and you just claim it as an in-kind contribution to your campaign. When you're campaigning, you may have some people who are going to say, "Hey, I have an expertise at developing mailers, and so that's my gift to you; I'm going to develop all your mailers. I'm going to take the pictures, and I'm going to put your marketing pieces together." Terrific! That didn't cost you anything.

You might have to utilize some unconventional resources. For example, you may know a student at the community college that wants to build their portfolio and is an excellent graphic designer. You may have this person work on designing your campaign logo. That might be something that costs you $100. I only have one caveat to using free and cheap services; Make sure that the work is of excellent standards. Don't just accept anything because it is free or cheap. You want to utilize and display great work because you don't want your campaign or your efforts to look really half-ass or cheap and cheesy. Don't let the price tag be your ultimate determinant.

Make sure that you follow your local state and federal financial reporting laws and regulations regarding accepting gifts/in-kind donations on behalf of your campaign. Please don't forget what I shared earlier about showing your appreciation to those who provide you with free and/or reduced-cost services.

Don't DIY – Get An Expert and Fill In the Gaps

You know, we have dawned on the age of where there are so many different coaches and consultants out there for just about everything in life. You've got life coaches, business coaches, political coaches, weight loss coaches, credit coaches, etc. You name it, and it's out there.

Through the many journeys of my life, I have embarked on and recruited a number of different coaches, consultants, and professionals to provide me with the guidance and support for me to reach my desired goals. I had a political consultant. I had a political fundraising consultant. I had a coach who helped me write and publish this book. I have a business/sales coach. I have a media coach. I have even had a business credit coach. The bottom line is, I have recruited a team of experts that have been able to fill in the gaps of what is needed for me to run a successful campaign and business. For example, I don't know a damn thing about accounting except for 2 +2 = 4. I'm not an expert at bookkeeping, and I'm not about to sit and waste my time trying to figure that all out because I don't have that kind of time on my hands. I'd much rather use my time engaging in activities that will allow me to expand my message and services to the masses, enhance my life, and build my business. I'd rather find creative ways of saving up the money so that I can hire an expert. And if we are holding to our honesty pact, in the end, I always end up spending more money when I attempt to do the work myself. You all know what I'm talking about. How many of you have started some kind of pet project with your car, your house, your apartment, the kid's treehouse, whatever the task (you get where I'm going with this)?

You went out and bought all of this different shit, and you're watching the doggone DIY channel on TV, or you're looking at Google University or watching YouTube College trying to figure things out. You end up just making a royal mess of things and the damn project ended up costing you more than it would have if you would have just had someone do it in the first place because now you have to hire someone to fix your costly mistakes. My point here is, invest in experts that will help expand your knowledge and reach. I am not saying that you need to spend every dime you have in hiring these experts. Be wise and do your research. Also, don't get caught up on, "I have to hire someone for every menial task." If possible, try to group up tasks required for your campaign with one professional, which could possibly save you some coins.

Again, hire people who genuinely care about your outcome. These are people who genuinely care about your mission. Both their and your goals and purpose should connect and be aligned in some way. Yes, you will pay them, but it will be for them to provide you with the expertise that you are lacking and need for you to be successful in your campaign.

Avoid the "Yes" and the "No" Folks

You're also gonna need to have a network of people who are going to be totally honest with you. I have a group of three to four solid women. My ride or dies. I call them my chin checking crew because these are the women who, no matter what I say, no matter what I do, they gonna give me the real. They're my cheerleaders, but they're also my teachers. They're also my coaches. Not the coaches in the sense of, who I pay. These are good friends who I have around me, and when I do something not in line, they have no problem with saying, "Tonya, you shouldn't have done that shit!" If the people you keep in your inner circle are only "yes" people, I guarantee you will crash and burn; and your success, if any, won't last very long. At least not in the field of politics because there are going to be times where you're gonna be so caught up in your feelings, so caught up in your emotions that you're not even going to be able to see, hear, or be open to even consider the alternative. You're going to be so passionate about a program that you want to implement, or you're going to be so enthusiastic about a policy that you've always been wanting to execute that you will naturally want to shut down any viewpoint that goes against yours, including from your own supporters. And you got naysayers or people who don't agree with you or your policy. There will be those that will be your naysayers who don't like you, will come against everything that you try to support or implement, and just for the simple fact that the idea comes from you. If you cannot deal with the fact that there will be those that just don't or won't agree with you, this is not the field for you. If you are one of those folks that are like Burger King and have to "have it your way," you will not be successful in politics. I don't care what capacity in which you serve, whether it's school board, city council, waterboard, congress, assembly; you won't be the only damn person at the table with an opinion or an idea.

When I served on the city council, I was one of five. So, there were four other people and me, who expressed five different viewpoints, had five different backgrounds, and five different belief systems. So, it was natural that there were going to be times where we didn't gel. There will be times where your colleagues and your constituents just won't get what you're saying. So, it is very critical that you have people around you who you can go to for mentorship and guidance, and who will be totally honest with you. They're going to give you the real. They're not just going to feed your ego or say something to make you feel good.

You need people around you who are going to be just totally honest with you about your behaviors. There's going to be times where you say something or do something that's out of pocket, and it'll be these folks who will say, you are out of line, was out of pocket, and you owe someone an apology. So, I have my chin check crew, and it's not a big group. That's what you need to have around you. Also, you can't have a bunch of negative people around you who never have anything positive to say about you, your passions, your ideas, and your visions. You need to cut them because they're not doing you any good. They're not your true supporters, and I'm not trying to be contradictory and saying, oh, only have people who like you around you or people who are only gonna agree with you. That's not what I'm saying. What I'm saying is you don't want anyone around that is going to kill your spirit. You don't want anyone around who's objective is to bring you down. Who's only objective is to make themselves feel better. The whole purpose is for you to grow. People need to do things out of love and if you continue to have people around, even people who are supposed to love you and again, that could be your mother, your father, your husband, your wife, sister, brother, hell, your kids, I'm not saying that you gotta turn around and then go to your husband and say, get your ass out of the house right now. Or to your wife and ask her to pack up her shit up and go. Unless you truly need to tell this person, "pack your shit up and go!" This ain't that kind of book. But you may need to say, "You know what, honey, I love you, but with this process here, I'm going to have to ask you not to be a part of it." Sometimes you'll just have to say, "I can't have you be a part of this because hell I want us to stay married." So, don't be afraid to exclude some people, and don't be afraid to include some folks.

You Have to Network and Speak Up

Campaigning is not the time when you develop a new habit of keeping to yourself. This will be the time where you will have to step out of your comfort zone boldly. If you have some restraints in going out, networking, and speaking to different people, you're going to have to implement some ways to get past those restraints. If you have a desire to serve in politics, you will be talking to people and all the time. You will be speaking to your constituents, your voters, your staff, your colleagues who you work with side by side, or other politicians in neighboring regions.

You will always constantly meet and speak to new people. So, it's so important that when you're out there, you are keeping an inventory of the people who you're meeting. Some of these same people will come to help and serve with you in building your campaign. These are people who you may call on three years later to serve as a member of your BADASS network. So, remember to always make a great impression and obtain contact information to include in your network database.

Since we are now close homies and are being honest with one another, making an effort to get out and network was very tough for me. I am what THEY call an introvert. I don't care to be in large crowds of people. I'm usually the one sitting in the back, scanning the room, and people watching. I'm the type of person that would much rather communicate electronically in the comfort of my own home. There were many times that I had to consciously be aware that I am like that and make a conscious effort to make myself be out and about publicly when it was warranted. If you are the one that's the life of the party, you may need to tone it down. If you are always obnoxious and loud, you may need to take two seats.

People Will Jump At the Chance to Help You When Your Motives Are Genuine

There is not much more to say here except for the fact that when your heart is in the right place, you have genuine motives in serving God's people, there will be many that will leap across boundaries to be a part of your campaign efforts. There are always many folks that are always looking for good people, causes, and campaigns to support. When I ran for office, I had people who I didn't even know that volunteered to help me get into office. The level of support from absolute strangers was pouring in like manna falling from the sky. People were just coming left and right, and I didn't even have to seek them out. I didn't even have to ask. I don't think that I received this level of support just because I was some fly black chick that said I was going to change the world. I believe the support I received had everything to do with my level of authenticity in truly wanting to be a servant leader. I ended up having a tribe of people who weren't just here for me, but they were here for the whole community. Many of these same people are around and ready to serve today. I can call on these same people and say, "Hey, I know this has nothing to do with campaigning or politics, but I need your help and support on something for a resident. I know you're into housing, and there is a woman over here that is homeless." These people are now a part of my BADASS network, and they have an expertise that's not only just to serve my needs, but also to help in serving God's people.

Chapter 4 - James Brown Was Wrong It's Not A Man's World

"Women make up more than half of the world's population and potential. So, it is neither just nor practical for their voices, for our voices, to go unheard at the highest levels of decision-making." Meghan Markle

Because of my political work, I am frequently invited to speak, teach, and serve on panels with the intention of increasing political awareness and engagement among women and girls. When I attend these events, the two questions that I am most repeatedly asked of other women and girls, is "How is it being a woman in public office, and how can I break into a field that is predominantly held by men?" Might I add that this question not only comes from just Black women but women of all races and all cultures? I truly believe this line of questioning is the fact that it's so very difficult for some women to envision themselves breaking into a position or field where they don't see very many individuals who look like them serving.

I know it's difficult. Not only is it difficult being a woman because there aren't a whole lot of women out there that are running and winning and serving in public office, and a lot of it has to do with the fact that enough women just aren't running. We won't use this time to fall into a woe is me moment, but to be real with ourselves and call the real truth out. The opportunities are available and not enough of us are taking advantage of them. Even with the insurgence of women that ran in 2018, there still aren't enough women running; therefore, the numbers of those women serving in public office will continue to be dismal. I feel that until the electorate on all levels is made up of at least 50% of women, and at least 25% of that are Black women, I won't be satisfied with the current percentages of representation. There are a number of reasons why Black women don't and won't consider politics. As I mentioned, the thought could be foreign as there aren't enough of us that are visual serving in these roles. Also, many feel that they don't have enough experience, are not young enough, are not old enough, are not worthy enough, and a plethora of other reasons, legitimate or not. The bottom line is we damn sho don't have enough Black women running. We do not have enough Black women stepping up to the plate and saying I'll have a run at it. And that has to change. Otherwise, we will slowly fade off as if we were never there in the first place. It's one thing to see trailblazing leaders like Congresswoman Maxine Waters and Congresswoman Ayanna Pressley flooding the airwaves, and we're like, okay, they are a dynamic force, but where the hell are all the other Black women? They can't hold it down or up on their own. They need the rest of us to step up and walk the halls with them. Let me be clear. There are a number of Black women running for and serving in various positions all across the nation, and we have never heard their names spoken. Those unsung heroes that fight the battles on our behalves, but aren't showcased in the media or the popular platforms. For those of you who have taken the brave step and are running and/or serving in any level of politics, I commend you, I pray for you, and encourage you to continue on.

Ladies, I challenge you from this very moment to start thinking differently. I want you to no longer take for granted who we have in leadership roles throughout our nation. Don't just focus your attention on the presidential races, or federal level races, or even just state-level races. I want you to begin to take notice and inventory of the leadership being held on every level. And I do mean every level. Who do you see serving in those positions? How many are held by women? By "GOOD" Black women? Then take an inventory of the great Black women that you know (don't exclude yourself if you identify as a Black woman) that would run circles around the person that is currently serving in the position. Now I want you to pick up the phone to call or text, email, Snapchat, DM, whatever your mode of communication; reach out to that woman and tell her that you think that she is dynamic and you would love to see her run for that position and that you would love to support her in her consideration in running. Now, lemme just say this. Don't be going out here, asking folks to do something that you are unwilling to support. This happens far too often and especially with Black women. The woman is pushed and encouraged to run, but when she makes the courageous decision to run, all the folks that pushed her disappear and part like the red sea. Don't do that. Be there from start to and after the finish, regardless of the outcome.

So, you have been sanctioned by me, and I am a persistent chic. I am going to keep riding you. When campaign season starts to roll around, you take a moment and think about your community, you start seeing those campaign signs going up in people's yards and on the corners; or if you happen to go to a city council or a school board meeting; and you begin to start taking inventory and you are looking like, I don't see any black women. I don't see anyone anywhere that even closely resembles me and can speak to the issues that are important to black women. "Houston, we have a problem!" Don't then turn around and say, "someone should do something about this." YOU be the change. YOU get up and do something. Nothing burns like a bad case of the drips than someone that wants to exclude themselves and to place the work on another.

If there is a small voice inside of you that says, I can do this. I can run. Then get up and run. You have what it takes, and so many women are intimidated by the fact that this is a male-dominated and predominantly white male industry. I'm here to tell you, yes, there are a lot of men at the table, but unless you get up and run, that won't change. Women need to be at the table. Black women needed to be at the table because I'm sorry, no man can do it the way that black women can do it. They just can't. We bring a different dynamic to the political table. We come with a different voice, and if we're not there, then our voice isn't being heard. It's been shut off, shut down, cut off, or nonexistent.

So no, it's not a man's world. They just want you to think that it is. I have had the pleasure of attending various meetings, events, and conferences on regional, state, and national levels of politics, and oftentimes, I was the only Black woman in the room surrounded by a field of men and usually those who are pale, male, and stale. Y'all know who I'm talking about. I often found myself being the only voice in the room fighting against the injustices that are plaguing the black communities and especially those specific to the demise of the Black woman. Don't get me wrong just because I'm a Back woman doesn't mean I only come to address the issues solely for black women. You know how we typically do it as black women. We care for everybody. We care for you if you're Latino, White, Middle Eastern, Asian, Pacific islander, etc. We don't care if you are a man, woman, or child. We don't give a who freaking ha. We represent all. And that's how I come to the table. I come to the table with a voice for everyone, male, female, black, or otherwise. Black women don't let someone shame you into not being an advocate for other Black women and our issues. There always seems to be a backlash when Black folks want to stand up for the betterment of other Blacks. Our motives and agendas always get called into question. We are always encouraged to shift our focus on helping the global, but our problems never get freaking addressed. The problem lies in the fact that we are not seeing the necessary actions for Black people and our communities being reciprocated among the masses that are currently at the political table, which have statistically been white men. Don't fall into the trap of letting anyone else define what advocacy should look like for you and tell you that you are a racist because you want to advocate for other Black people. I can't tell you how many Black elected men and women who refuse to support other Black causes or people publicly, just for the fact that they are fearful of what those who aren't Black will think or say about them. Bump that! The way I see it when these problems that have plagued the Black communities start to dissipate, I will shut the hell up, and begin to shift my focus and efforts on other issues. That isn't the freaking case, so I will be a mountain top advocate for the Black community and won't be shamed into not doing so. That is why it is important for us to be present, active, and not just sit pretty.

I have developed what I call the Tonya Burke 1:5 rule. For every one white woman that runs for public office, there should be five Black women running. Hell! One to five, five to one, don't get all caught up in the semantics. That's how y'all lose focus and start running on a tangent that is usually built on fear. I also have a rule that for every one white man that runs for an elected position, there should be ten black women running. We are a dynamic force. We are dynamic beings, and we have a voice. Our voice will never be heard if we're not there. If we're not in the room, our voice will never be heard if we're not involved in the process. And what did THEY say? If you're not at the table, you're on the menu. I say if you're not at the table, yo ass ain't eating and everyone that knows me is aware that I am a foodie and I like to eat. I eat well and not ashamed of the fact. If you ever took a look at my thighs and my hips, you will see that I eat really well. I have a doctorate in chicken wings, hot links, and peach cobbler. Need I remind you that this ain't no get healthy and get in shape book, so don't you dare judge me. Don't stall. Make your way to the table, just like you do when they call your table number to come up and eat at the family reunion.

Being a woman, and especially a Black woman, sometimes it will be a fight to get to the table. Getting there may not be easy. It wasn't easy for me. When I ran for city council, and when I ran for mayor, I was the only woman running and the only Black woman running, and I was called all kinds of "bitches." I didn't sit back and take the bull shitake that the evildoers were trying to slang. I also didn't let it deter me from doing what I needed to do. Stay focused. I knew that I was going up against a bunch of men and I also knew that I had what they didn't have to offer. I had a superpower. I'm a dynamic woman. I'm a dynamic Black woman. That's some extra flavor for your ass right there. Many of you are dynamic women but aren't walking around like you are the bomb.com. If you have to channel another great individual in order for you to get in this political game and take it by storm, then do so. If you have to see yourself as one of the BADASS chic from Wakanda's Dora Milaje army in the Black Panther, then please do so. Ladies, I know that was a fictional movie (they did use some true historical facts), but we need to be walking around like we have the power and can't anyone phase us. As my mother would say, "like your shit, don't stink." I don't care who it is you have to morph into Harriet Tubman, Sojourner Truth, Barbara Jordan, Missy Elliot, Beyoncé, Sasha Fierce, etc. Hell! Your momma, auntie Lola, or Deaconess Jackson from the church. Just do it already, and let's put these tired good ole boys out of commission; no need to discredit yourself because you're a woman and damn sho not because you're a Black woman. I have seen that second-guessing spirit amongst us for far too long, and it is time to kick it to the curb. You're not just good, remember you are the *S.H.I.T.- Sisterhood of Highly Innovative Trailblazers*. You can feel free to replace your 'I' with immeasurable, insurmountable, intelligent, intuitive, or whatever form of "I-ness" you choose. We have to push back against and kick off the doors of sexism, misogynism, and racism.

A few years ago, I was invited to sit on a panel of elected women that served in Riverside County, California. The panel conversation was based on the fact that there were very few women who served in any form of public office throughout the county. I believe that at the time of this event, there might have only been about thirty women serving in elected offices across the entire county. I was the only Black woman, and now that I think of it, the only woman of color that sat on the panel. So, you know how that goes, anytime we are the only Black person in the room, we have to speak for, represent, apologize, etc. on behalf of every Black or person of color in the nation. It was during the question and answer portion of the panel, a young woman from the audience, asked me, "How did you overcome the good ole boy network that has been plaguing this county and especially your city for decades?" My response to her and to each and every one of you is this: No matter who you are up against, do your homework. Learn their every move. Learn their systems, even research what the hell they eat every day. Once you know their plays, then you beat them at their own freaking game. You learn it so well that you play it better than them. One thing that I have learned about these good ole boys is that they are so braggadocious, arrogant and cocky. They run their damn mouths way too much. That is a good thing for you. You just soak up and learn what you need to take from them and flip the damn script.

44

You know you're going to have a lot of what I'll call punk ass men who are going to try to stop you at all costs because they are threatened by you. Threatened not just by your gender, but threatened by your black beauty. On the bright side, you will also have men who are going to move mountains for you to be in that position and serve in your purpose. One of my mentors, that's a part of my BADASS network, is a white man that has been there rooting and cheering me on before I even got into office. He is a former elected who knows the good old boy society very well, who was a part of the good old boy society but wanted to see something different. He saw the promise and the passion; that I was genuinely in love with the people of my city and wanted to see better for them. Did you hear that? I was genuinely in love with the people I was serving. He saw a level of authenticity in me to where he felt compelled to help me. I share this experience for you to understand that every man is not your enemy. Every person that isn't Black is not against you and can be down with your same agenda. Men aren't always going to be your foe. Some of them are going to be your friends, and you need to embrace that. This white man that I mentioned was one of my mentors through this political process and was not ashamed, not scared, didn't care about what anybody else had to say, had nothing to prove except for him wanting to see me be the best at what I wanted to be. That was his only intention. He frequently reached out to me and encouraged me to sit on boards and be in rooms of decision-makers that I would have never considered. He would often say, "Hey, have you considered being on this board? You should consider it. Outside of you being fully qualified, the fact that you will be the only woman and Black person are additional reasons why you need to be in a room. Here is a teachable moment for the others." He felt that these men needed to learn more about what it meant to be a Black woman living in our society, because they're having the discussions and making critical decisions about the things that are critical to people in the Black communities, but they don't have the experience, the expertise or the wherewithal to come to the table and talk about black people adequately. How and the hell can you address Black women's issue if you've never been a Black woman or have had any type of dialogue with a Black woman? Anyone can speak about us from the third persons perspective, but they will never be able to emulate our hearts and souls.

Brace yourselves; men will not be the only ones to discourage you during your journey. You know, sometimes, you will have other women who are going to try and discourage you. Hell, I had other Black women who were like, "No! You can't run, serve, or work in that position because you can't go into that circle with THEM; THEY don't allow us in that circle." It's not that these women were trying to do any ill or cause me any harm. They had just got caught up in the "sunken place." I call them political lost souls. Some meant well and were attempting to protect me, but they'd just gotten conditioned to that same old plantation mindset that we occasionally fall into as Black women. You know, "massah gone git you if he knows you can read," mentality. Those days are long gone, and we need to put that ish behind us. We don't have to stand in that. That's a choice. It's a choice for you to become what other people tell you to be. I chose not to. People throughout my life, not just now, have made an attempt to try and define who I am. It began during my childhood. I didn't take it on. I didn't wear that hat. That's not my persona. I didn't give a damn what they thought of me, and I kept pushing back against them. Most importantly, I kept showing ME differently.

Ladies, you're going to have to come and step up and go out for these positions, even when you're the only one. If you're doing it correctly, you won't be the only one for long, but you will be the first. As you are going along your journey, you should be cutting back those weeds for others to find their way after you easily. You're going to set it up, so it is easier for the next woman. Please! I ask of you and am somewhat begging you to lift up another black woman as you climb. One thing I absolutely and positively cannot stand is when I see Black women that have resources, who have game plans, who have all the things that other Black women have a need for, and intentionally keep that shit all to themselves. You know those heffas that say, "I ain't going to tell nobody. I just have enough for me. Everyone else will have to go and find this out on their own. It was hard for me, so it should be hard for her." (If this is you, shame on your punk ass!) That right, there is what I call a bitch move. And I'm not using the term bitch in reference to a woman. That shitake is shady, whether it's a man or woman. I can't stand these type of resource hoggers. You know, those people who will

46

steal, kill, and destroy to get all the resources, then keep all the resources to themselves; don't want to create opportunities for anybody else to get anything or heaven forbid get where they are. Those are the motherfuckers who don't stay in their positions for very long, or if they do, their asses are miserable and alone. Those are the ones who eventually other folks come after, and then they want to scream and holler, "Hey, my sisters! Come and save me! I'm all about Black women and Black women's issues." Hell to the naw you ain't! This journey is not a selfish one. This is one where we all should be taking care of each other. We all should be moving each other forward. This is not the time for you to want to go on and take on the position that you are the only one going to eat. You let "let them have cake" mother luvas are the ones I'm speaking about. I was doing my best not to cuss, but this is one of those subjects that gets me all heated, and my momma unleashes out in me.

Sisters, when you get in position and are serving with your male counterparts, make sure that you stand your ground and correct any level of misogynistic, racist, sexist bull shitake when it occurs. Don't take it out of the room with you, and most importantly, don't take it home with you. Treat it like a case of scabies and scrub down to not get infected. When not addressed properly, having these experiences can destroy us mentally, physically, and sometimes attack our positive spirit. There will be times where men will be dismissive of you, undercut your knowledge, skills, and abilities. And as O.T. Genasis said, "you need to cut it." I remember when I sat on a statewide committee and attended one of our regional meetings. I was the only woman that served on this committee and outside of the staff, and I was the only female committee member present. The chair had brought an item to the floor for discussion and asked for input from the members of the committee. I was the first to raise my hand but wasn't called upon by the chairperson. Pale, male, and stale proceeded to call on every man in the room whether they requested to speak or not. I sat there patiently with my hand raised, seeing him observing this fact, and ignoring me. Finally, I had enough of this display of disrespectful behavior, I got up out my chair, grabbed an unattended microphone and said, "with all due respect chair, I've had my hand up for the last 15 minutes. I'm now standing out of order in an effort to be able to have the floor and respectfully be granted the opportunity to speak as my male colleagues have been afforded such privilege." The chair proceeded to say, "Okay honey, okay, sweetie." See, that is where he royally fucked up. I ain't nobody's honey or sweetie. His name isn't Jason, who is my husband. I had to proceed to cut this fool at the knees. I responded by saying, "I am COUNCILMEMBER AND COMMISSIONER Tonya Burke, and you will not refer to me as anything else but that. I am not your honey, your sweetie or any other derogatory and sexist term that you feel entitled to use to address me." I then proceeded to make the statement that I had been waiting to make. A few of the other men in the room began clapping, and a few others rolled their eyes with disgust. The women in the room quietly cheered me on. I didn't care if there wasn't a sole person in the room that agreed with me. It didn't have any bearing on the level of respect that I had for myself and what I demanded of him.

Needless to say, the chair was totally embarrassed and turned beet red. He apologized and indicated that he was out of line for his behavior and statements. But if I hadn't corrected him in that forum and at that very time and in front of his male peers, he and they would have felt that it was okay to go on with business as usual. I just saw it as one of those teachable moments that my white male mentor spoke of. It also could have been a "snap, crackle, and pop your ass in the mouth" moments, had he not apologized, and corrected his actions. It was either going to be a teachable moment or that ass whooping moment. But I think he chose the best one.

You have to understand that even though you are the only one in the room, that doesn't mean that you're not needed in the room. God put you there to be the champion of that necessary change, to set a legacy, to make the crooked path straight. You are the modern-day Hansel and Gretel, dropping the crumbs on the way to grandma's house, so the next person can find their way through the forest. After I sat on that committee, I actively recruited other women to join in order for more women to add their insights and contribute to developing meaningful programs for all.

Chapter 5 - Say Bye To Felicia- Dealing With The Naysayers

"If I didn't define myself for myself, I would be crunched into other people's fantasies for me and eaten alive." – Audre Lorde

I guess we should jump right into it and start off with defining what a naysayer is. According to Merriam-Webster (2019), Naysayer: one who denies, refuses, opposes, or is skeptical or cynical about something. I want you to keep this definition in mind as we conversate throughout this chapter.[iv]

Never let someone's opinion of you define you. There are going to be people out there who are going to tell you that it's not your time to run. This is the one statement that I hear women of all races of cultures have been told when they expressed that they were ready to run. I can totally relate. Hell! I was told to sit my "black ass" down. You're going to be told that you're not the one for the job, that you're too tall, you're too short, you're too dark, you're too light, you're too uneducated, you're overeducated, you're not experienced enough, you're too boisterous, you're too fat, you're too skinny, you're too shy, you're too, too, too, too, etc.

Bottom line is you're not going to be everybody's cup of tea.

Nor should you be.

You may not even be a cup of tea. You might be like me, a nice glass of Moscato on a quiet afternoon or a Cadillac Margarita on a turn-up Tuesday.

You need to figure out who you are and stand in that, not worrying about what other people think of you or what they say about you while you are on this political journey. The problem lies when you begin to fall into believing the harsh words and lies that people with spew. You are going to have to be solid in how you feel about yourself and your identity. If you aren't, you will have a tough time trying to liv in your reality and not a façade.

This journey is one where someone will have something negative to say about you. It's just what it is. We all know how it is. We are in a time where we are able to sit back, peruse through social media, looking through our timelines at people posting and talking about politics. We are in a time where we can get instantaneous criticism and judgment from the masses. We see those keyboard gangsters that jump at the chance to viciously attack from behind the computer screen. If you, like my grandmother, always say, "wear your feelings on your sleeves," you are going to have a difficult time with dealing with this. I'm not one that takes joy in saying that certain negative behaviors come along with the territory or is a part of working within a particular job as if we should be accepting of this maladaptive behavior. Unfortunately, this has become the norm in the field of politics and quite honestly has become a new normal in our lives in general. The unwarranted and sometimes abusive rhetoric is more prevalent in politics than in any other field. I believe this is the case because typically in politics, one is elected by individual voters. And for some reason, people feel their voting power also provides them with a Willy Wonka Golden Ticket to act an ass towards elected officials. Elected officials work for the people, but aren't owned by the people. Therefore, no level of disrespect should be tolerated and accepted, from a constituent or anyone else for that matter. There are others that will tell you that being a public servant equates to being a slave. The devil is a lie and don't fall for that nonsense. If someone doesn't agree with you or your policies, you can't have a meltdown or fall into a temper tantrum. This is something that you will have to live with. You will also have to live with the fact that everyone will NOT like you. Hell, that's the case now. You can be the most loving, gracious, and stand up person; there is someone out there that's just not that into you. Again, that is perfectly okay, and you will have to live with this fact.

What I don't want you to do is to fall victim to trying to please everyone. You are allowing yourself to become someone you are not in order for others to support you. Don't do it. Be yourself at all times. Otherwise, you will be faking it until you make it for the rest of your life.

Your primary focus should be focusing on getting to the root of why you're doing this, why you want to change, and how you will make this change in your community. If you are focusing on why you want to make sure Daryl has clean water when he fills a glass and takes a drink from the faucet. You should be focused on why you want to stop a company from being able to dump hazardous materials on a site near a school. You should be focused on creating job opportunities for the most impoverished people in your district. These are all just some examples of the many things that you can be consumed with, as you are seeking to serve in office. When you are doing your job, and effectively, you will have many supporters who will love you. As I mentioned before, those who are in opposition tend to be the ones that are very visible and make a great deal of noise, but what matters at the end of the day are those who show up to the polls and vote for you.

You need to be focused on what changes you want to make in the communities that you are in and beyond because your reach is going to go well beyond just your community, district, region, etc... I am forewarning you that you will not remain in a small box or bubble unless you are intentional in your actions to do so. You may have in your mind, oh, I'm just running for a seat on a small water board, or I'm just running for school board in a small city, or I'm just going for an appointment on the planning commission or even school site council. In your mind, you may be thinking that it's small, and initially, it may be. But if you are a dynamic leader, your reach will go well beyond what you have ever imagined. That's a good thing. It also means that you will be exposed to more people. You just may not even understand how far your reach is going to go and what you're doing and that's why you can't spend any of your time focusing on what these jerks have to think and say about you because if you spend too much time focusing on that negative bunch, then you won't be able to spend your time focusing on serving.

You'll be too beat up. You'll be too distraught, and you'll be too discouraged to be able to implement anything that you've ever dreamed about implementing. So, paying attention to the naysayers is what you don't want to do. What you want to do is surround yourself with people who love you, who adore you, and I'm not just saying you don't take constructive criticism from people. That's not what I'm saying. I'm telling you to have genuine people who could mentor, advise, and support you. You cannot be cooped up with a bunch of those yes folks. You will not learn a damn thing by purposely placing yourself in a position where no one around you will question you and your ideas. You will remain stagnant if you just focus on having a bunch of people who just co-sign on everything that you say and do. If you don't already have, set out to build you what I call a chin checking crew. We go over this in another chapter. This will be one of your greatest weapons in the battle against the naysayers.

The naysayer's primary goal is to keep you from progressing. Their sole purpose is to do all they can to knock you off your game. It is important to know this upfront so that you can be very strategic in how you deal with these folks. Some of these naysayers are so vile, and they will do all they can to keep you from making positive changes, even if they are in a position to benefit from your work. Some of these folks won't know you, may have never met you, and may not even be aware of what you do. They could just not like you because you wore blue on a Thursday. Or that you ate wings on a Tuesday and tacos on a Wednesday. It can be a plethora of reasons why they are coming for you, but don't spend your time trying to figure that out or trying to win them over. Many of these folks are just bitter, and some have bonafide and deep-rooted issues with trauma, and you have become their scapegoat.

We desire more people like you that want to make that positive change, so forget what they're saying.

I remember when I first decided that I wanted to run for public office and let me tell you, it was not an easy decision for me to make. At least not initially. One of my greatest fears at the time was what are these people going to say about me. We frequently see political candidates get raked through the coals on a regular basis. We frequently witness them dragging the candidate's family into the mix, as well. Mommas, daddies, aunts, and uncles. Not that I have a scandalous family, I have always been a pretty private person, and my family is the same. I just didn't want folks in my business. If you are going into politics as an elected official, please conduct thorough oppositional research about yourself. You will do the same for your opponent but start with yourself. Check every last nook and cranny out there to see what is being said about you. Start with the internet. You can bet your bottom dollar that your opponent, well at minimum your naysayers will do so. If you know that you have some blemishes in your past, please don't walk around like you have a case of amnesia. Address and deal with it early in the development phase of your campaign. You and your team need to develop a plan on how you will approach it if asked. The last thing that you want to do is to be thrown off guard when the press reaches out to you about an issue from your past, or if a constituent asks you about it at a public meeting. Denial will not get you anywhere, but unelected. Sometimes things that have affected many people's lives will also affect yours, and it doesn't make you a bad person. You just want to be in control of the narrative and not sit back and wait for your naysayers to feel that they have one up on you and take your dirt and run with it. Hell to the naw! I remember during the development stages of my campaign, I was fearful of the fact that my past financial history would be called into question during my run for city council. My husband and I had previously filed for bankruptcy. We were both public service employees that took a significant cut in our wages as the result of being placed on mandatory furloughs. Through no-fault of our own, this caused us to lose approximately 40% of our regular income. When you're like most American families, living paycheck to paycheck; any amount of loss can cause your family to experience financial devastation. With one child in college, myself attending college, and another one scheduled to start college, we decided that the best option was for us to make some major cuts in our expenditures as well as file for bankruptcy. This financial strain that became a part of my life was also a matter of public record. Anyone that would pull one of those $12.99 background searches or just conduct some savvy internet phishing would come across this blemish. So, my campaign team and I developed compelling narratives around this issue, should it ever be addressed by anyone. Sometimes you will need to be the one to release the "story" before your naysayers have the opportunity. As I mentioned, it is better for you to control the narrative and be in front of the issue, rather than you being on the defensive and trying to justify or chase the story.

Please understand that it is natural for you to want to second guess yourself. Before I fully committed to running, I remember being concerned about what people would think about me. I started to fall into "am I good enough" or "will they like me," and even "can I do the job." I was quickly spiraling into the land of the Impostor Phenomenon A.K.A. Impostor Syndrome. The "impostor phenomenon occurs among high achievers who are unable to internalize and accept their success. They often attribute their accomplishments to luck rather than to ability and fear that others will eventually unmask them as a fraud (Wier, 2013)." Having a background in clinical psychology, I was very much aware of the Impostor Syndrome, but never did I ever think that I would fall into this web of self-deception. I had the knowledge, skills, abilities, education, expertise, and experiences that would make me a perfect candidate for the position of city councilmember. I could serve in the position, and well. The moment that I began to step forward and run, I began to second guess myself. Much of those feelings came from me worrying what others thought of me and the fact that when I began to verbalize my intent to run publicly, I started being met with opposition. It took my family, friends, and a whole lot of prayer for me to dig myself out of that trench. I flipped from living my life suffering in the Impostor Syndrome to taking ownership of the I'm the S.H.I.T. Phenomenon.

Your naysayers will have every reason under the doggone sun as to why you should not run or why you aren't the best person for the job. I was told that I was just too new because I had recently moved to my area a few years before deciding to run. My family and I hadn't lived there for a very long time, but I felt that I had lived there long enough. If I was there for one day, two days, one week, one month, or one year, it was long enough to know that changes needed to happen in my community, and I knew I wanted to be a part of that change. So, I felt like who are you to tell me what I can't do? I didn't make any inquiries to your punk ass, so why are you even talking to me? Don't get me wrong, everyone didn't meet me with closed arms . I had a lot of people who stepped up and wanted to support me. I had a lot of great people who are still on my team who wanted to support me, but I had a lot of people who also stepped up to ridicule me, lie on me, slander me, and plot against me. Just remember with all of these efforts to thwart me from having a successful run; in the end, I was victorious.

When I decided to run, I stepped out and did everything that the political campaign gurus suggest that a political candidate do. One important task that you will probably want to do when you run is seek out endorsements and support from various individuals, groups, organizations, political parties, and here's a big one, elected officials. Some reasons for gaining these endorsements: 1) Others to see that you have legitimate support from those that are considered to have an expert opinion, 2) To gain assistance with campaign resources. I want to interject here for a moment. Gaining endorsements is a great way for a candidate to advance their campaigning efforts further. Also, understand that you don't have to have endorsements in order to win your election. You can run a well-organized and well-received campaign without any endorsement and win. I am sharing this with you so that you don't feel that you don't have a chance in hell if you don't receive the endorsement of a party or an elected and your opponent does. Endorsements are great to have but are not a necessity. Do your best to secure them, but don't sell your soul in the process or give up your right kidney in order to receive one.

If someone you are seeking an endorsement from turns out to be a naysayer, don't spend much of your time and energy trying to convince them to support you. Spend that time nurturing the voters to support your campaign and to cast their vote on you. One of my greatest political nemesis and naysayer was an elected and his entire staff, who I sought to gain an endorsement from. This man and his political cronies did all they could to keep me from gaining the support and endorsements of other individuals, organizations, and the party. These entitled fools even attempted to contact the people who had already provided me their endorsements for my campaign in an effort to get them to rescind their support. They were not successful in their efforts, but child, they tried it.

But I reached out to some of the folks in my area, the local area because when I made a decision, I made it to run for city council.

I already said that I was going to win, and I already saw and set the vision that I was going to be the next councilperson in my city. So I set out, and I reached out to that person and I said, hey, I'm, you know, my name is Tonya Burke and I gave my little platform elevator speech (this is something that you will have to learn to do as a candidate running for office), and I said, hey, I would like to talk to you about my campaign. I'm running for city council in the city, and I would love to have your support, but most importantly I would love to share with you my vision so we can collaborate and see if my vision is in line with your vision for the area and possibly when I become councilmember, we could work together. So, this individual said he didn't feel the need to meet with me. He said that I wasn't important enough for him. Meeting with me wasn't important enough for him to engage in that conversation with me. But he would send a staff person to have that conversation with me. Needless to say, I met with the staffer, it was in the month of July, it was a hot day. I met with this person at a local Starbucks in the area and gave him my elevator speech and shared my vision and political platform. I talked about all the great things that I was planning to do in the city. I talked about some of the issues and the concerns that I had with the city and why I felt that I would be a great addition to the current council and why I felt that I was great for the position, but before I could really even finish my train of thought, before I could even put the "con" in conversation , this mutha luva cut me smooth off. For the sake of our dialogue, we're going to call this fool, Remy.

Remy cut me off and said something to the effect of, "Looky here, I hold the political power here in this region, and I am the one that makes all the decisions for the elected who you are trying to seek an endorsement from. And so, I naturally said, well, great, you know, ain't no need to deal with any middlemen. Let's cut straight to the chase, cut straight to the person that is making the decisions. And then he went on to say, and you know, no one can get to this elected unless they go through me.

And I said, terrific. I'm glad I'm sitting at the table with the person that's in charge. And then he looked at me, and he said, and I have never forgotten the words that he uttered out of his mouth even though it was over six/seven years ago, but I remember it like it was yesterday. I don't remember it because it's caused me to experience any pain. But I remember it because it taught me a great lesson. This a**hole went on and had the nerve to say, "The elected who I represent will never, and I mean never, ever support you because you're not the right one for the position." Initially, you know, my big audacious smile that I had on my face turned to, uh, I wasn't frowning, but I gave him that look, you know, that look you give somebody who's sitting in front of you, and you're asking yourself, what did this mother luva just say!?

I gave him one of those looks, and I said, excuse me, can you repeat that? And he said that shitake again, I proceeded to inquire as to why I would not gain the support of the elected. I then found myself creating a list of faults to try and justify his reasoning for coming at me like this. You know, I was creating this false list of why I wasn't good enough, which is something I shouldn't have done. He didn't even bring up the things I was listing, but I brought them up because it was like I was trying to give him a pass on why he wouldn't want to support me. Ladies, do not do this to yourselves. Don't ever give someone reasons as to why you aren't worthy or good enough. Me doing this was me displaying the symptoms of the Impostor Syndrome. Just know that if you are not supported, you are still worthy.

In disbelief, I continued on riddling through this laundry list, and he said, "No, that's not why we will never support you. He said I just want to help you out. I just don't want you to continue to waste your time because you're a very smart woman." See conniving a**holes will try to discredit you, attempt to insult you, and then give you a compliment all at the same time. Don't fall for that shit. This is a "backhand compliment" if you can even consider it a compliment at all.   This is that fluff and bull they dish out, so they can send you on your merry little way and feel good about themselves. This was the point where I should have ended the conversation, thanked him for his time, and left the meeting. But I didn't. I kept on asking questions and making statements attempting to inquire what I did wrong, prove my worthiness, and gain an understanding of what I could do to be accepted by these idiots. But he still wouldn't get to the point. He talked about how society has a problem with women in politics and how society is not supportive of women of color in politics (mind you this man and the elected that he represents are both men of color). Now I am reaching my boiling point with this man and his shenanigans and was pissed beyond pisstivity.   I was tired of his rambling and doing what my momma refers to as "talking out of both sides of his neck."   You know what I mean, double-talking? When someone says one thing and the next word, they utter contradicts what they just said. This is what he was doing for the last 15 minutes of our conversation, and I didn't have all damn day for him to tell me why they weren't going to support me. I was starting to get to the Samuel Jackson pissed point of where I was like if this mother luva doesn't just come on out and say what he means. So, I did us both a favor, and I said, "Can, you say what you mean and mean what you say?"

He said, "Let me just give it to you straight. You live in a city that has a population of over 70 percent Latino and only eight to nine percent black. You're Black." He proceeds to look at me and is holding his hands up like, don't you get it? And I'm sitting there looking at him like, okay, and what else? Then in a snarky tone, he says, "They're Latino, you're Black, and there are only a few Blacks in your city. They're not going to vote for you. No one is going to vote for you because you're Black and the wrong type of Black. The city already has another Black woman on the council. They'll never have too many of

58

you in the same position. We're looking to support a Latina woman because that's what the people in the city would want." I asked his ass if they conducted some kind of poll in the city? And he said, "No, no, we just have a pulse of the community, and we just know that other Latinos are not going to vote for those who aren't Latino." I asked, well, how did the Black woman that's currently in office get voted in? Mind you, this same Black woman elected has been winning every election and is currently the longest-serving councilmember that the city has had. He said, "that was a different day. She's been on the council for a long time, and that was a different day. So, she's like a unicorn and an exception to the rule. Plus, this will probably be her last term, because she will get voted out." Let me add that this Black woman elected went on to win another re-election. I'm looking at him, you know, wanting to jump across the table and snap, crack, and pop his ass in the mouth because he was totally out of line. This man didn't know shitake about me, and he was judging me based on what he chose to focus on, which was my race and skin color.

I had enough and was ready to shut down this nonsense. I told him that I believe that people in general vote for candidates who they feel have the same values as them and who want to make positive changes in their communities. I didn't believe that the people in this city are any different than the rest of the world, and most voters want people in office who will listen to them, be a voice for them, and create policies and programs that's of benefit to them. And I don't believe that my race or my gender should even come into the equation in regards to my fitness for duty.

And this fool went on to say, "You just don't get it. I was trying to be cordial to you. We're not going to support you, and that's just it. And no one else is going to support you because they know that no one will vote for you. You're just the wrong type of Black." I knew that I was sitting across from somebody who had a belief system that I didn't believe in. I was sitting across from someone who really didn't have a pulse on the community, who really didn't give a shitake about the community because if he did, he would want the best person for the job. He would care more about my qualifications. He'd care more about my experiences. He'd care more about my education. He would care more about what it is that I can bring to the table to improve lives as opposed to trying to destroy mine.

So it was at that point that I flipped the script, and I said, "You know what, thank you for this interview or this conversation or whatever you see fit to call it, but I'm letting you know that I've made a decision that I am not going to seek your boss' endorsement. I have that choice as well. Just as much as you have the choice to give me an endorsement."

Ok, I am going to divert for a moment. This message is to those electeds out there that have these staff folks on their team out there running around as if they are the one that was elected into the position. These a**holes will be the death of you and will cause you to eventually end up out of your position. Sit these folks down and keep them from playing kingmakers or get them the mental health treatment that they are longing to have for their insecurities

I would be lying to you if I told you that was the last time, I had similar conversations. It was organization after organization. It was person after person who essentially said the same thing to me. You're too Black, or you're too 'fill in the blank.' There are going to be people who may come and tell you the same thing. But I ask you, do you believe it? That's the most important piece here. See, I didn't believe any of that shitake this man was trying to slang my way. He was trying really hard to slang that nonsense. He was slinging that shitake at me like a dope dealer slanging crack, but I just wasn't buying what he was selling. I knew who I was when I stepped into that meeting and I knew who I was when I left that meeting. I knew who I was going to be serving in that position and that's why I was able to go head to head with that naysayer and every other one out there. Yes, I was called a nappy-headed nigger, jigaboo, etc. The devil is a lie.

You cannot base what a few people say as the norm for all people.

It didn't matter what any of these a**holes had to say about or to me. There are many that I have witnessed in this political game, attempt to disown who they are to gain acceptance from their naysayers, especially those that hold powerful titles. I didn't flip the script and change who I was. No, I didn't leave who I was at the door. I carried who I was into each and every one of those meetings throughout the campaign trail. I didn't show up as anyone else. I showed up as Tonya.

You're going to have the naysayers. You're going to have the critics, and people will hand out opinions like Halloween candy. You have a choice on whether you act on what they say about you or not. I chose not to act on any of those people's negative opinions. I'm asking that when you are in this position, when you are ready to take that plunge, when you are ready to step out there, enter your greatness, and run for public office; I want you to remember that you need to say bye to Felicia. At the end of the day, I ran against all the odds and naysayers, won my race, and got more votes than anyone running. Ironically the same assholes that fought against me ran around town, taking credit for my win. Now ain't that some bull shitake.

There is always going to be at least one Felicia that shows up in your life. Perhaps your naysayer may not be named Felicia. Maybe Tony, maybe Raphael, maybe Julie, maybe Michael, maybe Mark. Who knows who it could be, but whoever it is, there are times where you're going to have to give these people the metaphorical middle finger (you may even feel a need to give them a real one), remain in who you are, stand in that greatness, and keep pushing forward to serve the people who you're destined to serve.

Chapter 6 - Show'em Better Than You Can Tell Them

"Deal with yourself as an individual worthy of respect, and make everyone else deal with you the same way." – Nikki Giovanni

Ok, we have reached the halfway mark. Remember, we agreed to be honest with one another. We said that we were going to do things differently. We are cool homegirls that are going to be real with one another. I hope that I haven't scared you, but have empowered you. I don't want to set you up for failure, but want you to know any and everything that you may face out there so that you can be appropriately equipped for the journey. You would be totally pissed off with me if I invited you to a party that I was hosting, told you it was a costume party, when, in fact, it was a pool party. Here you then showed up in a hot a** pirate costume when everyone else is wearing swim attire. You're sticking out like a sore thumb and everyone looking at you as if you may have a few tools missing out of the toolbox. I don't want to have you out there ill-prepared for what will be the most invigorating and powerful moments of your life. I'm not one of those sisters that will let you walk around with a monster booger in your nose and not tell you it's playing peek-a-boo with everyone that sees you. Then go behind your back and talk about how foolish you look. No, ma'am! We aren't going to do that to each other. We are going to be honest with one another, and do it with love.

Now that we got that out the way let's just dive right back in.

There are going to be many, many, many times, and as a black woman you already know this, of where you get to talk till you're blue in the face and sharing with somebody about your skills, your abilities, your gifts, your expertise, and the things that you do well and people just don't take you seriously.

There are times where you are going to have to just show them. There are people that are going to doubt you. There are people who are going to doubt what you can and can't do. There are people who are going to tell you that you're not the right fit. There are going to be people who tell you that it's not your time. There are people who will tell you there's no way in hell; you will win that race. That's what I was told. There's no way in hell that you're going to win that race. I didn't just, you know, take that and runoff in the corner or go to my room and hide behind the door and get in the bed and cry and sulk. I looked those assholes square in the eyes, and I said, well, it looks like I'm gonna have to show you, and that's what you're going to have to do too. You are going to have to show them better than you can tell them. Sometimes there'll be times where you're going to be discredited. There's somebody out there that's going to say you don't have what it takes to do what it is that you're trying to do. You're not going to be able to serve in whatever capacity you're striving to serve in and what position you're going after. That's fine. Or even if you're someone that's not necessarily running for public office, but you're helping someone else run for public office. If they don't say these things about your candidate and they'll say things about you too, you're going to have to show them. Don't spin your wheels trying to change people's minds about you.

Don't spend all your time trying to beat a dead horse as they say. Don't spend every breathing moment of your life-changing things and your campaign efforts or changing things once you even get into office and trying to prove to somebody who you are. The only person you need to believe in is God, and He already knows you're worthy to hold the position. He already knows what you're capable of. He already knows that you are great. You need to believe in yourself. You don't have to prove it to anyone, and when I tell people, show them better than you could tell them, I'm saying, just do the doggone work. Get out there and do the work. Get out there and serve your community. Get out there and create policies that change and improve lives. Get out there and create programs that take individuals, organizations, and agencies to another level.

Get out there and be a change agent. These are things that you're going to have to do in order for you to be successful. You just have to. You have a purpose. You have a mission. You have a vision. If you don't have any of those things, then you will have to get to the point where you have them because they're going to be what's going to guide you and keep you on task throughout this process. You're going to have to go out there like you're the baddest chick that EVA' stepped on the planet, and I mean the baddest one. Badder than your momma. Badder than your sister. Badder than your homegirl. Badder than the baddest of who you think you are. You have to take that mindset and go out there and say, I am the baddest and I have a voice. Even if this chick over here don't get my voice, even if this jerk over here is unwilling to hear my voice, I have one, I have a mission, I have a vision, and I'm going to succeed at it. If you don't have that mindset, you're going to be defeated.

You're not gonna be able to do anything that you set out to do if you don't have a winning mindset. People like to be around and be associated with winners; Including you. So, know that you are a winner regardless of the outcome of your political race. Hell, you don't have to win. You could lose your race and still come out a winner. I ran for the position of mayor of my city in 2016, and I didn't win that election, but I walked around like I was already in the position that I was going after, and I still do. Not that I'm trying to be in a position and take it away from the person who's in it, even though if I truly wanted to, I more than likely could, that's not my thing. But I did walk around like, I got my S.H.I.T. together.

I told you earlier that I am the S.H.I.T.

Black women, you are the S.H.I.T., so you have to act like it.

You don't have to be conceited, but be confident. There is a difference. Because I feel that way about myself, I have other people who radiate towards me who want to be a part of that S.H.I.T. that I am speaking of. Once you have mastered this, you then take some of your BADASS S.H.I.T. and share some with another woman to expand her S.H.I.T

You get what I'm saying?

No one wants to be around you if you are walking around with your head held down all the time, feeling sorry for yourself, acting like woe is me. And it's not just about, oh, I've got to have approval. You don't need approval from anyone but yourself. You got to be like Beyoncé "I woke up like this." FLAWLESS! I don't mean show'em in the way of proving or begging folks to understand who you are. Hell To The Naw! What I'm saying is feel free to being okay with letting someone check out your backside when they doubt you. You're going to be unfazed by the bull shitake and keep pushing and moving on and doing what you need to do. Come on now. I know I am not the only one walking around like I have a bomb ass backside.

Honestly, not winning that election in 2016 was one of the best things that happened in my life. So many things changed, and not because I went into the whole thought of, I was a loser, or I was defeated. I'm telling you that I went on like, I had won, because I am still serving, still doing the work, still improving lives, but I never took on the role of defeat- Never did. I don't say that I lost, I say that I learned. And, if I hadn't run that that race. I wouldn't be here right now, writing this book for you all to read. I wouldn't be here right now, writing this book, encouraging you to run your race and win.

I don't care where you are in this process if you haven't taken the step to say yes to yourself, then no one else will. If you haven't taken that step to believe in yourself, then no one else will. And I'm sorry, but you know, you're going to have to walk with the attitude of I'm the S.H.I.T You're going to have to be in the zone of I am here. I have a mission; I have a purpose. There's nothing or no one that's going to get in the way of that. And fuck anyone who can't support that concept or is doing everything in their power to keep you from being successful. Many women I have met, they say, I don't want to get my feelings hurt. Hurt feelings are inevitable. They are going to get hurt in this process. If you can't get past this, then this journey may not be for you right now. You see, I didn't say indefinitely. I said right now. Remember we're being honest with one another.

Because there are times where you will cry, there will be times where you will be happy, times where you will be sad, times were you feel joyous, and even times when you feel triumphant. But even with all those emotions, there will still be times where you're just gonna feel beat up – not by others, but because you're beating your own damn self-up.

Self-defeat will cause you not to fully support yourself or anyone else. How do you walk in the room? Do you walk into a room like you are the fine ass chick in the club? That's how you have to act. Like, my momma always said, "I know my shit don't stink." That's how you have to be poised and know your shitake don't stink. You're the best one for the job. You're the best one doing the job.

And all of those who think something different, say what you need to say. But I just showed you something totally different than what you've been saying or what you thought. I even had people telling me, "it's a waste of your time to serve those types of people who you're trying to serve. I was totally appalled because I'm like, I'm one of those people. You can't go in with that holier than thou attitude feeling that because you are going into public office, you are better than the people you serve. You are the people who you serve.

I was told that I wouldn't be able to have the opportunity to complete many of the goals that I was able to accomplish. You know, I had people telling me, "You will never ever, ever implement a program in your community where people can get a free college education." One of the reasons why I ran for public office is because my city has some of the lowest educational attainment than many of the other cities in the region. Less than 10 percent of the people in our city have a degree or have an education higher than a high school diploma. Only around

10 percent have higher than a high school diploma.[vi] I'm sorry, that equates to unemployment, to crime, to poverty, to a number of other issues that many never look at to see the full picture and never make the connections. So, you may think you're going in there to work on one goal, but you will end up working on a number of other things because they're all interconnected with other issues in the communities.

This was on my goal list, and now it was done. I, with the help of a great team (because it it takes teamwork), created a program where people who live in our city are now going to be able to obtain a bachelor's degree and for free. Do you know how significant that is and especially when you live in a community where a great deal of the people is living below the poverty line. Now they can go and get their bachelor's degree and increase their earning potential in their household, to now be the model for their own children. Their children can now look at their parents and say, "okay, now my mom or my dad have a bachelor's degree and I can strive to get one too." These parents are now setting a new trend for their families.

You see what I'm talking about?

How one of your ideas or goals can change the lives of millions and for years to come?

These were the so-called experts who told me what I could and couldn't do and what I was going to be able to do. I will say about 100% percent of the items that I had on my wish list, on my to-do list, on my campaign platform, every policy, every program, every initiative, everything that I listed I was able to accomplish in my first term. I was able to accomplish about 80% of my goals within the first year and a half to two years of my term because I was determined to be that change and wasn't going to allow what others thought about me or my abilities stand in the way of progress. What you set out to do will be a people-driven mission and not driven by your ego. Once your ego intrudes and takes precedence in your work, you will jeopardize the success of the outcome.

After two years, I was able to start working on other things that I probably would have started working on in a future term. Even when the experts tell you that what you want to do can't be done, proceed to do your own research and if it can, have the wherewithal to say, "I'm going to show you better than I can tell you because I've been telling you all this time and wasting my breath." Don't spin your wheels, wasting your time, when you can be out there actually doing the work. So, say to all of your naysayers, "sit back, relax, don't trip, and allow me to not only show you how it's done but show you how it's done right."

Chapter 7 - Step Out Of Your Comfort Zone, Leap Into Your Greatness

"Embrace what makes you unique, even if it makes others uncomfortable. I didn't have to become perfect because I've learned throughout my journey that perfection is the enemy of greatness." - Janelle Monae

To sit up here and have this conversation with you all, my girls, and put the idea out that I didn't have some level of fear and doubt when it came to my consideration of running for public office; if I told you that I came and I stepped out the gate from the jump Gung Ho, ready, being an awesome BADASS that was going to take on the world, I would be the biggest damn liar on the planet. I will tell you right now that I was scared as hell. I was scared. I was fearful. I doubted myself. I was like a Doubting Thomas. Let's just say a "Doubting Tonya." I'm going to keep it 100. I didn't come out the gate automatically feeling 100 percent confident or 110 percent.

I didn't see myself as great. I didn't feel like I had any form of greatness. You know how you hear so many other people talk about how great you have served in different capacities. Whether you serve in your church, your school, whether it's in your job, your community, hell while shopping at the local Pic n Save wherever you are. I know that you have people who come up to you all the time and tell you that you are great. They talk about how great you are. They talk about how much of a benefit, an asset, and how special you are. And when it came to this whole political thing, that all went out of the window for me. I had been so comfortable in the shoes that I was wearing. I had worked them in, I had busted them in, and I had been in them for years. I was so comfortable in wearing the shoes that I had been accustomed to wearing. See, I have particularly always liked to wear flats or shoes, with just a tad bit of a heel.

I don't do the doggone stilettos. I don't like to wear anything that has more than ½ or an inch of a heel. Throughout my life, when I started to wear higher heeled shoes, I would start to wobble. I don't walk gracefully in stilettos. And then on top of all of that, I have this fear that I'm going to fall and bust my ass in front of people, those who I shouldn't be busting my ass in front of. So, I don't like to wear any other types of shoes besides those that I'm familiar with and comfortable with. Stepping into the figurative new shoes of politics, caused me to have the same feelings of placing my stubby toes into stilettos. This reminded me of a time when I had to attend an event that required me to get all dressed up, and I had to wear a ball gown. Unfortunately, wearing this gown would require me to have also to wear shoes that I wasn't accustomed to wearing. I would have to wear those types of shoes that were higher than an inch. Oh, hell to the naw is what I thought.

The length of the dress that I had to wear to this event required that I wear shoes that had the height to accommodate that dress. I had to wear heels that wouldn't cause me to step on, snag, tear or rip the hem of the dress, and put holes in it. With much resistance and reluctance, I ended up having to wear some shoes that I initially wasn't comfortable in. I didn't just jump in these new heels, throw the ball gown on, and run off like Cinderella at the ball. I tested the new shoes out. I took my time and practiced wearing them. I first put my feet in them, adjusted the straps and I stood up in them. Gurl! When I stood up, my legs and ankles were wobbling and trembling so much so that I sat my a** back down, kicked those new shoes off, and vowed that these death traps weren't for me. I don't know how the hell some of you wear these damn stilts on a daily basis. Have mercy!

I gave up.

I began to talk myself out of even wanting to attend the event because I didn't want to step out of my comfort zone. I didn't want to do what it would take to go beyond my fears and conquer wearing those shoes. It wasn't until I took another look at that beautiful dress, and I'm saying, "You have to do this, Tonya."

If I wanted to wear that gorgeous gown that was made just for me, I would have to put on those shoes. As a couple of days had passed, I attempted to put the shoes on again. I strapped them up and put them on. I stood up in them and was a little wobbly, but not as wobbly as I was before. Then I took a few daring steps in them. They felt a little slippery. So, then I quickly sat back down, took those mutha luvas off and was like, this shitake just ain't for me, I can't wear these shoes. These shoes are just not for me. These bad boys were meant for somebody else to wear. You know Beyoncé and them can wear them, but I can't.

But then I looked over there at the dress again. That gorgeous dress that was specifically made for me and had my name on it, I would never be able to experience wearing it, because of my fears. So, I decided to try practicing walking in the shoes yet again. So, the next time, and the next time, and next time, I walked a little bit further and further in those shoes. I practiced walking in those shoes to the point whereby the time it was time for me to wear that dress, I was able to put those shoes on, and I felt so comfortable. I was able to skip, I was able to hop, but I wasn't able to run. I ain't gonna sit here and tell you I was running in them damn shoes. I ain't running in nobody's stilettos. I am not a fool. But I was able to put those shoes on to the point where I was able to put the dress on and comfortably walk.

I was able to cut a rug, do a little dance or two. You know the electric slide, the cupid shuffle. Come on now, come on. Don't act like you don't know that every time we have a barbecue, a graduation party or retirement party, a birthday, a wedding reception, a baby shower, you name it; we find a reason to do the electric slide, the cupid shuffle, and all of those different line dances. I was able to partake in all of the fun and dancing and in those shoes. I promise you that I'm not telling you all of this because I have a desire to talk about clothing and breaking in brand new shoes. But I told you all of that just to say that I had to get over my fears in order to step out of my comfort zone and leap into my greatness. I have had to do some of the same things in other areas of my life that didn't end with me having to wear a dress and stilettos. The point that I am making is that we will undercut ourselves in order to remain comfortable and stagnant. And here's that word again, FEAR. I was fearful of putting those shoes on because of all the undesirable visions and negative things that I thought would happen to me if I wore those shoes. I made the assumption that I would never be able to wear those shoes, and if I didn't wear those shoes, I would never be able to wear that dress that was made just for me.

See, if you don't step out of that comfort zone and leap into your greatness, you are never going to be able to fully live the life God intended for you. That life that He sewed perfectly just for you. He took your exact measurements to where your life perfectly fits your arms, your neck, your breast, your hips. It's perfect, just for you. No one else can get in it and wear it like you can. You will never be able to live that life You can wear other dresses, but you just won't ever know what it's like to experience wearing that one. The same can be said of life, you will have a life. you just won't have a full one if you don't step out of your comfort zone and learn to wear and walk in the shoes intended for you. You're going to go through some experiences that are going to prepare you to be able to live that life that God intended for you.

I'm not saying jump off the cliff without a parachute and just expect yourself to survive.

Now, I don't know about you, but I know a lot of people who always say, "Oh - God, got me." He is just going to take care of it. Yes! God will take care of you, but he also has given you a brain to use and make decisions. God didn't make you no fool either. He has given you different tools. He's given you different things in life to where you can survive. If you are fearful, if you are scared, you are never going to get there because you're never going to take that chance.

Before I finally decided that I would step out of my comfort zone and pursue politics, it was other people who came to me and saw the greatness in me that I didn't initially see in myself. I was so stuck in my comfort zone. You know, I had been a career and vocational counselor for umpteenth years. I was comfortable in that role. I knew every area of this profession like the back of my hand. I was more than willing to own that greatness. You know what? I take that back. I hadn't even worked the full level of my greatness in that position. I was living in the fact that I know how to do this job, but the fierceness of it, I didn't quite own it. I knew it, and I knew it well.

It was a girlfriend of mine, Yvonne, who came to me and said, "You know, Tonya, you should run for public office." I looked at her, and I said to myself, "Negro, please! Naw, not me. I ain't the one. Not with this mouth that I have. I wasn't built for that. That ain't for me. Plus, I don't know how to do that." Yvonne hadn't even known me very long, but she was able to spot out some of my great talents, skills, and abilities. She would often hear me talk about making positive changes at my job and my community. At this time of my life, I was a steward and heavily involved in the union where I held membership. Yvonne had the opportunity to witness me taking action without me second-guessing myself or my abilities

My go-to excuse: I'm not into politics. I'm not a politician. Let me tell you that this political message didn't just come from Yvonne. It was like Jesus was on a mission to drill into my head that I should run for public office. No, really! He actually was. After this initial discussion with Yvonne, the flood gates opened ,and all types of folks began to approach me with the same message of running. I started thinking that the CIA was bugging me or could I have been suffering from delusions and, people were reading my damn thoughts. I didn't know what was going on because it was person after person, after person, after person, after person who kept approaching me and saying, Tonya, you should run for office. And I was like, this is a mutha luvin conspiracy.

Each and every time I turned my back to the thoughts and suggestions presented to me. I dismissed the idea for a very long time because I was like, that ain't me, I don't have those skills. I can't do the job because I'm not equipped to do the job. I'm not smart enough. I'm not good enough. I will have to make way too many changes to myself to be ready. You know, all of the negative things started coming latching on to my very existence.

It wasn't until I had a conversation with California State Controller, Betty Yee, and her husband Steven that I had a light bulb moment. I was attending an event and sitting alone, away from everyone being my usual introverted self. There were all these political folks attending the event. They were all networking and doing the things that you do when you're at events, and your goal is to make connections. I was cool with just people watching because that's what I do.

I'm a counselor by trade. So, I've gained those active listening skills over the course of my counseling career. I sit back and watch people. I watch their behaviors and listen to what they say. I don't do too much talking when I am wearing these antennas. I remember one of my council colleagues described me as being methodical. He said that I am always sitting back watching, listening, and carefully examining the situation. I have a feeling it wasn't his intention to describe it as one of my positive traits. I believe this was one of my traits that probably irritated him. Okay, back to the story. I was at this event, sitting alone, people watching when then State Treasurer Yee, approached and asked me what office I was running for? I quickly responded, "Oh, I'm not going to run." She then gave me a strange look. What I didn't share was that this event was specifically held for those women who were a part of a political training and planned on running for office. I talked myself into being a part of this training, would go through all the motions, hear everyone out, but deep in my heart had no intentions of running for office. You know how we do it. See an ad for a seminar, tell ourselves, "I'll go and see what they are talking about. But I'm not going to buy shit." That's kind of what I was thinking.

So, I went, but I had to step out of my comfort zone because this was a circle, a group of people that I wasn't familiar with. This was a circle and a subject matter that I had not entrenched myself in before, and I felt out of place because I was going there in the sense of wearing a politician hat. And it just felt very uncomfortable for me because I didn't see myself as a politician and to be quite honest with you, I still don't. And so, Betty asked me, "Why won't you run for office? What is it that's holding you back?" I responded by stating, "There's nothing holding me back. I'm just not a politician, so I can't be in politics if I'm not a politician." I figured that response completely got me off the hook, and this woman with this big, bright, bubbly smile and great disposition will be turned off and just walk over to the next woman who was in attendance because she wanted to be a politician. But luckily, for my benefit, my response didn't influence her to scurry about. She just stood there flashing that smile I was speaking of earlier. In one of the most soothing and calm voices that you can imagine, she said to me, "Well, that's terrific that you're not a politician because that's not what we need."

And then she went on, asked me where I lived, what I did for a living, you know, and then we had a discussion about the people who I have served in my career, how long I've been doing the work I was doing and how my work has benefited others. Just when I thought I had provided all the information that she needed, I had satisfied Betty's curiosity on whether or not I was a hack, and she now knew that I didn't have the experience to carry out a role in politics. Nope! I was so wrong. We just transitioned into a conversation where I expanded on my characteristics, qualifications, and education. And it was a rundown of what felt like some sort of resume but not just a professional resume, you know, it was just a rundown of my life. At the time, it felt as if this conversation took a few hours, but we had only spent about twenty minutes together. At the close of what one would describe as an interrogation, Betty said, "You will be perfect for this role because we need more individuals that care about the wellbeing of people, and their primary focus isn't just about politics. All that you shared shows that you're the perfect person to serve." At that very moment, I was the one that ended up displaying one of the biggest smiles.

You know the kind of smile where your jaw muscles end up aching?

And it was also at that very moment where the light bulb clicked on because I'm telling you that my figurative living room was dark. It was as many of us say pitch dark. You know how dark a room is when you enter in from an area that is extremely bright, which makes the room seem even darker than it truly is. Your eyes can't fixate on any bit of light, and you ain't got your smartphone so you can try to, you know, navigate your way through and you're slowly walking through touching and trying to reach for furniture and trying to reach for things to guide you to where you're trying to go so you can turn the light on so you can see. You find yourself blundering your way around the room, hoping that you don't stub your baby toe. Y'all know the baby toe is the one that always takes the hit. That's where I was. I was in there walking in the dark, stubbing my baby toe on everything that I was walking into. Graced by trying to get to the light and turn the light on, that light came on. It was at that moment when I fully understood the greatness I needed didn't need to come from a textbook, it wouldn't come from a get rich quick seminar, or even from a self-help book.

It was always there in me.

There's a difference between a public servant and a politician. [vii]

A Public Servant is about people whereas politicians are about politics - and I'm NOT here to make you a politician. I'm not here to help you be the best politician. I'm here to help you be the best public servant who serves people in the field of politics.[viii]

I just needed somebody to help me realize that. I recognized that and gained a greater understanding that God sent Betty to help pull out what he had already started. Well, what he already had inside of me. It was at that moment where I knew in order for me to do this, I had to get past my vision of what I thought a politician was. And I had to get out of that feeling that I needed to morph into someone else in order to be a politician. I could feel comfortable in just being me and still in order to do this thing that terrified me, in order to serve, in order to improve lives, in order to help people, in order to change circumstances for the better, in order to mentor, in order to guide, you know, we've got a lot of titles for people who do that. Teachers, lawyers, doctors, ministers, they all should have the same common goal, and that's to serve people, and so once I got past that, I decided to step out of my comfort zone and take that step in that direction.

Don't get me wrong, yes, in order for me to be the best that I felt that I needed to be and going in and running for office, I sought out as much information as I could.

I'm a reader, an avid reader. I love to read. I don't always have time to read, but I love to read, so it's the first thing I did. I jumped on the Internet looking for information on how to run. I thought how do I do this? How do you run for office? And that's just the technical skills side of running. I realized that before I could even get to the technical side of the running, I had to do the inner work and get a handle of the mental side. I had to set my mindset that I was already a winner. As I say, those of you who are in coaching and those of you who have been a coach, those of you who are in therapy, you understand that term inner work. I had to do the inner work, and it didn't require, you know, it didn't require me to have all these different skills, talents, education, in order for me to get the right mindset.

Yes, God, sent timely vessels by using people like Yvonne, Betty, Flo, James, Ricardo, Alan, Linda, Valtina, Alexis, my husband, children, parents, and host of others, just like I'm trying to be a vessel to you at this very moment. In order for you to understand and know that your greatness is already there within you, it is you. You are great, everything about you: the good, the bad, the ugly, and the indifferent. Everything about you can serve you well if you strive to bring the good out of every part of you and your experiences. If you're going to have to take that step, you're going to be required to do some things that you're not used to. Speak to some people that you don't typically speak to. Go to some places that you don't necessarily want to go to, but should. It's going to take you to read some things that may be beyond what you are accustomed to. It's going to require you to do some stretching because you can't grow if you aren't stretching. Your knowledge and experience chest will have to get bigger to be able to accommodate every new person, place, idea, thought, information, and perspective. All of that new stuff that will be soaking up inside of you will no longer fit in that same little box that you have always put yourself in. That same little box that you allowed others to put you in. If not, you will just end up with a busted-ass box.

The great thing about stepping out of your comfort zone, it's gonna make you a successful candidate, a successful leader, a successful councilperson, a successful congresswoman, a successful assemblywoman, hell, a successful president. Because I foresee, in the near future, that we will have a president that is a woman that is Black because we got too many dynamic and sho nuff showstopper black women out here, who are ready for the position. Not enough of us have a vision expansive enough to see ourselves in the position. They don't see their greatness in being able to serve on that level.

I work with candidates, helping them develop into their best selves, and developing the right mindset in order to be able to run, to be able to win, to be able to serve and to be able to be successful and stay in office. Anyone can look up how to run a campaign online, check out a couple of videos on YouTube, and run a damn good sho nuff of a showstopper campaign and win. But the difference I've learned from working with other candidates, is that when you work on the whole being and not just the campaign, you have greater success before, during, and after the campaign. Most of the political consultants out there and reading materials just focus on the campaign. A good campaign will help you get there, but the campaign won't keep you there. The campaign won't help you be successful once you are serving on the job. See, I want to make sure that you're ready for the position, that you don't step in unprepared. You want to implement a plan and program that will give you the knowledge, skills, and also massage, nourish, and pamper yourself for growth.

You can get there without all of these things as you can see, there are many that have. Not taking on a fully comprehensive approach can definitely open yourself up for some unnecessary struggles and that won't make you feel like your best self. I remember the day like it was yesterday when I decided to take a leap and finally applied to a training program that helps train women to run for public office. Earlier, I shared with you about how, at the time, my girlfriend Yvonne provided me information about the training program. When she suggested that I apply, remember I told you when she left the room, I threw that damn application in the trash. Deep down inside, I knew I wanted to take the chance and apply. Everything that I said out my mouth supported a desire for public office, but my mindset said something else. My mindset said something else because I was afraid. My fear kept me from taking the step and passed on what could have been my only opportunity to have access to some top-notch training. If Yvonne had come to me and said, "Hey chickadee they have this great program for career and vocational counselors, I would have jumped at the opportunity with no questions asked. I would have taken the time to complete the training even though it probably wouldn't have further progressed me along in my career and probably would have just kept reinforcing the same shit that I already knew. Thus, leaving me to continue to be stagnant. It would have just been another action and activity that I would engage in to make me feel good. To make me feel like I was doing something. We tend to do that.

Remember, I said that God found a need to have some of the same folks reach out to me the following year and recommend that I apply for the program. So that following year, Yvonne approached me with the same conversation, "Hey, the training program is accepting applications again, and I think you should apply. It's like the Harvard and Yale of political training." I thought to myself, Shit! If it's the Harvard and Yale of political training, I'm definitely not the one they are going to want. Now mind you, if she said it was the Harvard and Yale for counseling, I would have been cool with that because I'm like, I'm a shoe-in. But she said Harvard and Yale of politics. So, you see, I was hung up on that word politics when she said politics that was my trigger to shut me down. I said, all right, then I won't get in. This time I verbalized, I said, Yvonne, please stop talking about that because that's just not me. And then she said, why not you? Let them tell you that they won't accept you. How about you apply for it, don't be afraid of being denied, but how about you apply for it and see if you get in and make a decision at that point.

See, I used to be one of those types of individuals that would fight towards my own demise if it meant that I could prove you wrong. I will challenge you at all costs.

So, I got all of my information and documentation needed for the application process and applied. After I completed that part of the process, then the thoughts of me not being able to get anyone to write

79

recommendations for me began. And I knew that was a doggone lie. I knew Yvonne, the person who was pushing me up to applying would provide recommendation number one. I then began reaching out to other friends and colleagues and asked if they would provide me with a recommendation. I didn't think that I would get any responses or would get major push back. To my surprise, I had recommendations pouring in, and I only needed two. I reached out to 20, 30 different people because I said, okay, I ain't gonna get anyone to be able to write one for me for this, not for politics. I received between 20 and 30 recommendations from my friends and colleagues. Each and every last one of them spoke from the heart and talked about me in ways that I wasn't even willing to talk about myself. They saw me in a light that I didn't even see myself. They prophesized in those letters about how they saw me serving in politics, and that blew me away. It blew me away. I turned in my application, received the application confirmation, completed the interview for the training, and was chosen for the program. Now mind you, there's only a handful of spots available in the training. Only about 25 spots are available for this program, and there were hundreds of women all throughout the state of California who applied to be in this program. And I was chosen.

And then I thought to myself, what if I wouldn't have been afraid and would've applied the year before? None of that really mattered because it was at this point that I decided that it was time to kick rocks at fear and uncertainty. Long story short, went to the training program, learned everything I could learn about running a top-notch campaign, and actually started to see myself in the position, actually saw myself serving as a councilperson. I surrounded myself with so many people that spoke positivity into my life and not against it. When you're in a development phase, when you take on new things, you need people to tell you the real. Why would you run to the very people who always speak negativity to you? That's just another form of self-sabotage. Why would you go to people who ain't never had nothing nice to say to you? Who never supported your plans? Never thought anything great about you? Who has always been critical, ridiculed, and chastised you? Why would you do that? Why put yourself through that?

So, I took that leap of faith and met some new and brilliant people, learned some new skills, gained some new knowledge. Sometimes it takes you to take that first step to come out of your comfort zone, and then you'll go and fill in the gaps by meeting the people you need to meet and learning the skills you need. The moment I graduated from the training program, that was the very moment I started my campaign to run for public office. Yes, throughout the journey, I was met with naysayers. Yes, throughout the journey, people told me what I could and couldn't do. Yes, throughout the journey, there were some who didn't see what those other people who were behind me saw, but none of that mattered. I got out there, I ran the race when I finished that training program, because I took that leap of faith because I trusted in God to be able to put me in a place where I knew he wanted me to be, to step into my destiny, to go in the direction of my purpose, and I felt okay with that. I knew he was moving me into my greatness by me taking that one step that I was afraid of. I developed the courage, and I knew in my mind that I would be a winner. I knew in my mind that I would win, so I didn't just run to run. I ran to win. I won my race.

So, now it's time for you to step out on your faith, run your race, and win.

Chapter 8 - Stop Keeping Up With The Kardashians Run Your Own Damn Race

"Trust yourself. Think for yourself. Act for yourself. Speak for yourself. Be yourself. Imitation is suicide." – Marva Collins

You will find throughout this whole process you will make the daring decision that you want to serve, become a world changer, and that you want to be the one to make the change that you were destined and born to do. You will find that through this process, you will be compelled to want to do what someone else has done or what someone else is doing. You will also be compelled to want to mirror everything that you see, and I just want to warn you to proceed with caution in doing so. You'll have a lot of people who are going to tell you what they did and then you'll jump on board and say, well, you did that and was successful, so I'm going to do it. There's nothing wrong with, you know, getting sound advice. If there's a foolproof method in achieving some tasks and it works for you, by all means, do it. There's nothing wrong with that. Why reinvent the wheel if you don't have to? It will be very difficult for you if you do not obtain consultation and pick up some information from those who are experts in the field and have done this time and time again. There is nothing wrong with getting a blueprint for a successful campaign. There's also nothing wrong with veering off from the path to a certain degree and walking in your path. See the problem lies when you're trying to keep up with the Kardashians, y'all know who I'm talking about. You know how we see the Kardashians? You're striving to have the same things that they have, just because it's possessed by a Kardashian. For example, Kylie has a pair of shoes, and you think those are some bomb a$$ shoes. You are going to go to hell and high water to try to find yourself another pair of those shoes, and you damn near went bankrupt buying them. Driving all around town and trying to find those shoes. And then you went bankrupt because you didn't realize that she paid $5000 for those shoes. You had to come to the realization that you didn't want to pay $5000 for a pair of shoes, but you wanted them so bad just because Kylie has them, and they look good on her. Then you decide you want to wear them. The same doggone shoes that you just spent $5000 on plus another $300 traveling all over the world looking for them. Now you want to put on those shoes. You put them on with this dress you envisioned them with, and you then realize that you don't even look good in them. They looked good on Kylie, but they look a hot mess on your wide feet. See, I'm trying to keep you from spending all that money to not even look good and what you're spending it on. I'm trying to keep you from keeping up with that damn Kylie and those damn Kardashians. You feel not you. Child, if it's not the Kardashians, it'll be someone else. Keeping up with everyone else can cause you to lose yourself and possibly all of your coins.

Just in case you didn't hear me the first time, I will say it again. In doing so, you will lose yourself in the process. Politics is one field where you can easily fall into becoming a totally different person. You will have a number of people who are going to be tugging and pulling at you, telling who you should be, what you should have, what you should look like, how you should walk, and how you should talk. They will stroke your ego to get you to be who they want you to be. You will have to be comfortable in who you are, be your authentic self, and always continue to have your authentic voice. When I was elected into office, I had so many people who came to me and tried to tell me who and what I should be. I didn't have a problem with that.

I had some folks telling me I should wear my hair a certain way or I should wear a certain style of clothing. I'm a very eccentric person. I am one of those, bamboo earrings at least two pair, sitting on the bus stop sucking on a lollipop. I'm one of those what L.L. Cool J considers an around the way girl. Always have been and always will be. Being so doesn't discredit who I am, and you being your authentic self will not discredit who you are either unless your authentic self is a thief. The constituents who voted for me voted for the authentic me. They didn't vote for the façade of what others wanted me to be. They didn't vote for who I was portraying to be. They voted for the authentic me because that is who showed up each and every time, I knocked on their doors and asked for their votes.

That was the same authentic me that showed up each and every time, and it didn't change. Once I got in office and raised my right hand, swore to uphold the law, and serve the citizens, I haven't changed one bit. I'm not going to change because I know how important it is for me to be me, just like it's going to be very important for you to be you.

You know what they say?

Do you Boo? Because if you don't do you, you will lose you in the process. You will forget who you are. You forget who you were. You will become something that you're not, and you won't be successful because eventually, people are going to figure out that your portrayal is a fraud. The fraud factor will rear its ugly head and others will no longer trust you. They'll be like, who the hell is she? She's not the person I knew. All because you were trying to do what someone else was encouraging you to do or you were trying to do what you thought you needed to do to play the role.

I mentioned before that I could be a very eccentric person. I like to wear bold, bright colors and not the traditional dark browns, blues, or black. There are times where I do wear my hair naturally, permed, and short edgy styles. I am not shy about wearing my hair in a multitude of colors. I was chastised and discouraged when I was running for office, from being my authentic self, with the fear of me not looking "political." I had some "experts" telling me I had to have a certain look in order to be successful in this arena. I was thinking to myself, what the hell do my clothes have to do with me doing what I need to do to improve lives? What does my hair have to do with me doing what I needed to do to improve lives? My ultimate goal was to get elected into office and help improve lives. I could do that with blonde streaks in my hair. I could do that wearing an orange suit. Which I ultimately did.

Everything I did was according to me, my personality, my style, and it was according to what I felt. My style and appearance are a reflection of how I feel about myself. Allowing someone to dictate that part of me is the same as allowing them to tell me not to be a woman or be Black. I was going to rock what I felt good in. Not what Candice felt good in. Not what Michelle felt good in. Not what Stacey felt good in. I was only concerned about what Tonya felt good in. Now, don't get me wrong, I'm not telling you to go out there looking like Bozo the Clown. That's not what I'm saying. It's not what I'm saying at all. What I'm saying is don't change you. You are who we need, and you are who we want. Yeah. There may be times where some things about you may need to be a little polished. You know? If you go to a dinner and you don't know if you grabbed the glass or the fork to the left or the right. Table Etiquette. Yeah, you don't want to show up in public places burping and farting in front of your constituents. That's a matter of displaying bad damn manners. You will learn appropriate protocol on how to conduct yourself in political meetings by following Roberts Rules of Order. This is something that you can learn, but if you have a desire to actually abandon yourself in order to succeed in this position, you will fail.

So, don't be so busy looking at someone else's life. Don't be so busy and trying to emulate what someone else is doing, how they talk when they are at the podium, and how they deliver their speech. I met a council member that was frequently referred to as the "New Barack Obama." He spent much of his time attempting to present himself as if he was President Obama. It didn't go over well, and he always appeared as a fraud. Just always continue to keep you in the equation because the people are reaching out to you, and that's who they want. They want you. Not who others think you are. If they want someone that isn't you, there is nothing that you can do to win these folks over, unless you plan on spending your entire life perpetrating another identity. That can be very exhausting.

Even your friends and/or family may give you advice to drop parts of your positive personality traits. When I started out in politics, I had a good friend of mine that had good intentions, suggest that I somehow morph into a white woman in order to be successful. I looked at her like she was crazy. How the hell was I going to do that? Here I am this dark-skinned Black woman with a natural do. I didn't think that her plan was going to go over very well. She further clarified that I needed to "act" white. She felt that taking on white mannerisms would allow me to climb higher up the political ladder more efficiently than if I was my regular ole black self. You're going to have a lot of people who love you, come to you and tell you to abandon you, all while feeling they are doing it with love. They mean well, but I want to keep telling you that an opinion is just that, an opinion. You have choices. When people give you their opinion, you have the choice to say thank you, but I'm going to keep being me, and that's exactly what I did. My friend encouraged me to dull down myself and my personality. She said that I was a "little too loud." And I said, what do you mean loud? Because I'm not a loud person in regards to the tone of my voice, so I'm looking like, what the hell is she talking about? She was like, I mean, in your appearance, you know, when you come into the room, everybody's looking at you because of the loudness of your clothes and your hair. And I said that's terrific! Because when I come into the room, I stand out from everyone else in the room and I'm memorable. I thanked her for her advice and took a pass. I didn't curse her out, and I didn't get upset with her. I just realized that she was trying to put off her insecurities about herself as a Black woman onto me. I have my own shit to work on and can't be taking on anyone else's.

I remember attending a political meeting with this same friend, and I wore a BADASS fuchsia suit. I wasn't wearing what many in my region would consider a traditional political hairdo. I didn't step into the room as Condoleezza Rice. I stepped into the room as Tonya Burke. And when I stepped into the room as Tonya Burke people radiated towards and remembered ME. Not the person who my friend wanted me to be. These folks at this meeting realized that they'd seen me in other settings. I probably wasn't even dressed the same or even remotely looked the same as I did the time that they initially met me. But when they saw me again, my name registered with them, and they said, "Oh yes, you're the one I previously met at such and such event, and you were wearing that beautiful fuchsia suit." The entire time I've served in politics, and even beforehand, that's just how I've always been and not that it's purposely done. Not that I'm purposely setting out to be different, but I am different, and I embrace my differences. There isn't another person out there like me. They can try to be me, but will never be. I'm the only Tonya Burke like me on this planet, and no one else is exactly like me. Like no one else is exactly like you, and that's why it's so important that we have you. That's why it's so important that you continue to be you because you're the one that God created the way He created you.

He didn't create you to be Michelle Obama, Condoleezza Rice, Maxine Waters, you know, those are some bad women. And when I'm saying bad, I mean in a good way. They are members of the BADASS women crew. As bad as they are, they ain't you. You have your own level of BADASSERY that they don't possess. That's just the way God intended it to be.

Just stay in your own lane. Have you ever been driving down the freeway, you see a cute little car that you like, and it pulls up next to you? You know, for me, that's the Maserati Quattroporte, that's my dream car. One of these days I'm gonna get my dream car. Any time I see one on the road it's like I fall into a trance and engage in a starry-eyed gaze. I'm like, oh my God, do you see that beauty? I want one of those cars so bad and staring so hard that I start to veer out of my lane and into their lane. I then feel foolish and have to quickly snap back into my right mind and swerve back into my lane. I damn near hit that beauty that I love so much because I'm staring at it so hard.

We do the same thing with other areas of our lives. Keep your eyes on the prize and stay in your lane. Keep your eyes on the road and stay in your lane. Be focused and driven on your path and not someone else's. Like I said, you don't want to keep up with the Kardashians. You don't want to keep up with the Jones', the Browns, the Greens, the Clintons, or the Obamas. They're not for us to keep up with. We can admire and do so from a distance but don't become a carbon copy or a copy cat.

Don't be a forgery in your own life.

Don't be an identity thief. They are locking folks up for stealing identities.

Be you and be the best you that you can be. Be you when others don't even understand you. Be you when others don't even like you because that's just gonna happen. There's gonna be people who want to look at you and find fault. You're going to do your best to impress them, and they just aren't going to like you. What was that movie called? 'He's Just Not That Into You.'

You're just going to be dealing with a large number of people in politics, especially with voters. Don't be surprised when they love you one day, and then the next day, they can't stand you. It just comes along with the territory. Don't take it personally and keep doing a great job in serving those same folks who have expressed hatred towards you. God will make your enemies your footstool. Allow Him to fight these battles in winning over these folks. The harder you personally try to make them like you, the more they will dislike you. As I said before, your supporters will sing your praises from the rooftops. We're here today having this conversation because I want to keep you from having to go through some of the trials and tribulations that I went through.

Whatever you do, don't leave you at the threshold of a door every time you approach one. If you are a dark-skinned Black woman, be proud to be a dark-skinned Black woman and don't leave you at the door. If you have a medium complexion or light complexion, don't leave you at the door. We come in all shades and all sizes and should be proud of them. We come with all types of knowledge, and this world needs each and every one of us to play a part in it to be the best that it can be. I need you to keep doing you boo. It's that's simple. Don't flinch for a second, even if the guilty culprit means well. Some of them will be your mother, your father, your best friends, but then some people are going to just be haters. Just damn outright haters who want to see you down and who want to stop you at all costs, to keep you from doing what it is that you are here to do. The devil has a lot of minions out there, and they're going to be trying to keep you from doing what you need to do, keep you off your game and distract you by showing you or telling you that you're less than, is one of the ways that it's being done.

You're not for everyone, nor should you be. God created billions of people, so if someone can't connect with you, they got billions of other people who they can connect with. Hmm. Isn't that a thought, you can't be everything to everyone? You will kill yourself in the process trying to do it, and I don't know about you as long as I'm living on this earth, I want it to be a good life, not one where I'm always worrying and spending my time looking in the mirror in shame because I see myself, but I don't want to be myself. A Kardashian is who I never want to be.

Chapter 9 - This Journey Started The Day You Were Born

"Winning is great, sure, but if you are really going to do something in life, the secret is learning how to lose. Nobody goes undefeated all the time. If you can pick up after a crushing defeat, and go on to win again, you are going to be a champion someday." – Wilma Rudolph

Oftentimes we feel that our past is a hindrance to our future. What you may not understand is that the beginning of this path that you're trying to go down didn't begin today, last week, last month or last year. This necessary journey that you may not even have a clear understanding about started long before you even formulated a thought. Everything that you have experienced in life. The trial, tribulations, and triumphs have been preparing for you for this present time. Your journey started the day that you were born, actually when you were conceived, but you just didn't realize it. That's when your journey started. When God decided that you were going to be a physical and human being, he planted that seed into you. God has had a clear vision of where you are going. This vision includes your possible decision to run for office and you wanting to win. As you can see, I added the thought of you winning because when you run or go after anything, when you run for public office, you better damn sho run with the vision and the mindset that you're going to win. If you don't, don't even bother with wasting yours or anyone else's time trying to run any type of campaign. If you run any race with the thoughts that you're going to lose, then you certainly will. If you run with the thoughts that you're truly gonna win, you're gonna win. You may not necessarily win the campaign, but you're gonna win.

So, when you make the decision that you're going to run for office, and you're, going to win. When you make that decision, every journey that you have gone on throughout your life is going to help you get there. Initially, you may not feel that your background and your history are worthy enough to get you in the bathroom, let alone a leadership position. There isn't a moment, there isn't an experience, there isn't a trial or tribulation, there isn't a heartbreak, there isn't anything that you have endured in life that won't contribute to you getting there, everything in life that you have experienced including birth is a part of this journey that's going to get you into public office, that's gonna get you in that seat, and that's going to help you be successful once you get in there. I need you to trust me on this one. I have met with many women during my political career who have expressed a desire to want to run for public office, but so many of them come to me and say, "I have a terrible past." I have told each and every one of those women never to count themselves out or discredit themselves. Taking a full inventory of the good and the bad will be the first step in that direction. I say, yeah, your past, because it is what's going to get you there.

These women always doubt and ask how their past is going to get them into office when it has been a bit sketchy. They even question when they have a squeaky-clean background. You may not have the best upbringing, or the best Mama and Daddy. You may not have lived in the best neighborhood. You didn't have the best car. You didn't have the best education. You didn't eat the best food. You didn't wear the best clothes. You didn't marry the best spouse. You didn't have the best finances. You didn't have the best kids. All of that is what you are going to tap into. All of that is what you need for your journey.

Everything that you have endured and experienced from the point of conception to now has all played a part in that journey. He carefully and meticulously crafted you for this position, for this role.

Yeah, things may not have been the best, and you may not have been at your bestI met a young lady who didn't have the best childhood. She was actually quite ashamed of her entire past. She had been sexually assaulted at a young age by her father, her brothers, and her uncle. Every man that she ever cared anything about betrayed her. Every man that she looked to for protection, every last one of them violated her. Her mother knew about it, told her to keep hush, and to move on because that's what many Black women do. We are quiet about the sources of our pain and move on with our lives even though we are broken . That's what this woman did, and she kept that bottled up for years, and as a result, she never dealt with it in the healthiest way. So, she started to deal with it in unhealthy ways.

She started drinking, started using drugs, started living a promiscuous lifestyle, sleeping with men who she didn't care about, and who didn't care about her. This is what she was unconsciously taught as a child when she dealt with what she dealt with and being sexually assaulted. So, she went on, had one child out of wedlock, two children out of wedlock, finally three children out of wedlock. She wasn't married to any of the men that she had her children with, and she wasn't with any of the men who she had her children with. Two of the three men ended up in prison.

One of the men ended up being shot and killed because he was involved in drugs and gang activity. So, at a point in her life, she decided that wasn't what she wanted anymore. She wanted to live differently for her children. She said that was her goal, her children's happiness, and success. She went back to school because she had dropped out of high school. She went back to school, got her high school diploma and enrolled in community college. She did exceptionally well in community college, graduated with honors, and went on to a four-year university. She did exceptionally well at the university, graduated with honors, and set out to make the best life for her and her children. She's now married to a wonderful man who loves her. Here is a woman that made some wrong decisions in life. I spent years rehabilitating and rebuilding and have all of the receipts to prove it. But she was afraid to allow herself to move on. She was afraid to allow herself to reach her highest potential. Here's that fear word again.

She was afraid of that journey that she went through and overcame. See, she was still stuck in that place. But she wasn't still stuck at that moment. She went through the journey. She learned from the journey. Doing so allowed her to grow. It made her a stronger person. She's a better person in this world because of that journey.

But she told me, "I just, I can't run for office because of my past because I'm damaged, I'm blemished. I'm stained. And if anyone found out about my past, they would crucify me. I can just see it, see the headlines, you know? Old base head running for Congress." A congressional seat was what she wanted to strive for. Now when I say a BADASS, this chick here was a BADASS like you've never seen a BADASS before. She'd done so many great things for so many others and without recognition. And she wasn't even asking for any. She just did it because that was her God-given gift and because of her love for other people. See, she had just been out there doing the damn thing, being an overachiever, you know? And she didn't see any of the positivity, she was stuck in her past, and had determined that based on other people's perception of who she was, how she should be and what her past should have been. But you know, I told her, I said, "why wouldn't you run for office? I think you're a perfect person." And she wondered why if elt that way even after she had just shared that she was "damaged goods."

And I said, yeah, you in all your bags in my best Erica Badu voice and I am not a singer at all unless it's in the shower. When I'm in the shower, that's when I am the best damn singer in the world. I sing in the shower, I don't sing in the choir, I don't sing anywhere else. I sing in the damn shower, and when I'm in the shower, I am the best damn singer on the planet and nobody can tell me anything different. So, you ain't about to tell me anything different today. But in my best Erika Badu, singing voice "Bag lady. You gon' miss your bus dragging all them bags like that.[ix]" I mean, that's truly where she was. She got all these bags of her past that she has been dragging around from place to place. She got the bags of the men who should have been her protectors. She got the bags of her mother who should've been her champion but wasn't. She's got the bags of being a teen mother. She's got the bags of having children with men who didn't make the best decisions in their lives. She's got all these different bags. The school dropout bag. The promiscuous bag. She's got the fornicator bag, you know, she's just got all these fucking bags. She can't continue to carry all that she's been carrying and hold it together. But she hasn't been carrying them, and now her arms are hurting. She's dragging. She was doing what many of us do, and that's trying to seek redemption from man and not God. If you ask, God will forgive you, and He is all that matters. Man will always hold you in a higher regard than they are willing to hold themselves.

That's what I told her. I said, you know, I think you're a perfect person because who can go into politics and talk about drug policies for our nation better than somebody who knows firsthand, who has experienced the devastation first hand. I mean, come on for real who will be better at creating policies and programs for teenage mothers than someone that was a teenage mother. Who could go in and create programs and policies for sexual abuse survivors than someone who has had that experience? So, I advised her not to disown, discredit, or denounce herself. Her experiences may not have been the best, but they are a part of her that she can't go back and change. Your past experiences may not be the best part of you. But it is a part of you. Who is better, who would be better to do all of those things than someone who knows firsthand? You didn't have to go to school to learn about it, you know from firsthand experiences. You are the expert. You have a unique expertise, but you are not owning it. You do not even own the expertise of the education that you may hold. And don't get me wrong, you are not alone. I have had this same struggle myself.

I have chosen to live with my past, but not in it. The point is for you to be optimistic and to strive to see if there are any positive aspects that can be drawn from your past. I'm telling you, once you get to that point, you don't just stop growing and learning. You know, you just don't become stagnant. This is a forever evolving process. This is a forever evolving movement. God intended for it to be so you could get to this place. And that's it. When you run, and you win your office, and you get in that position, mark my words, I guarantee you will not stop there. You will know things that you never ever conceived or dreamed of. I would've never thought that I'd be sitting here right now having this conversation. It was never in my mind, never my intention to do the things that I have been doing since I've been in the game. Since I have gone into public office, I never would've thought I'd be where I am now doing the things that I'm doing and going in the direction I'm going in. I know that everything that I have endured in my past, that journey that I have had from the date of conception. It has all played a part in building me to be where I am today, and it will continue to contribute to my future.

You know, I didn't have the same experiences as this young woman. Nor have I experienced what you have. I can never walk in your shoes, but I got some broken and busted stilettos, sandals, hush puppies of my own. I have some of my own baggage. I, too, faced teen pregnancy, abusive relationships, food addiction. I know what it's like to have to sleep on the floor in the dark with no lights, being called welfare "queen" (some of the assholes I went to college with named me welfare queen, because I was a single mother of two kids putting myself through college with my babies. No worries those same folks are posting old pictures sharing how they knew me way back when and sending me messages saying we always knew you would do great things. Heffa please!), low income, project housing, disbarred from school, I know what it's like to have to go and beg to be on the welfare system so you can take care of your children. I know what it's like to be ridiculed and dismissed and dogged out because you're doing your best to try to take care of your children. I've been mistreated, used, and abused. I've had to file for bankruptcy. I have a child that's diagnosed with a disability. I can go on and on. I've had some trials and tribulations. Not the same as you, because of my journey. My role in this world is not the same as yours. We have different roles, and there are different expectations of us and serving them within our own purpose. That's why it's called your calling because it only belongs to you. I'm living in my purpose, so stop looking on my side of the fence. My grass may be greener than yours, but your grass is fuller than mine. You get what I'm saying? I took all that shitake with me to the council and will take it with me one day when I get to the white house.

My shitake ain't supposed to look like yo shitake. So, we both had a journey although different, but we both had some blemishes in our life that we're not all power to the people about. The difference with me is I'm at a point in my life where I don't mask any of that because it's been those very experiences that let me know I was the perfect person for the job. It's why I knew I could be the voice for the people because I was able to go in and speak to their truth. I was able to go in and sit at the table and not fake the funk, not, you know, operate a facade. I was actually able to be and continue to be the real deal at the table while being okay with bringing my stuff with me.

As Badu says in her song, I collected all those damn bags all those years. The difference now is I don't drag them all over town with me. I have them neatly placed away. My bags are neatly stacked like the towels in the linen section of the department store. I used to work at Montgomery Wards as a teen, and I have some stories to tell you about working in the linen section folding all of those damn towels for someone to come and only tear them apart. If you can't relate to the towels, how those neatly folded, crisp dress shirts that are perfectly stacked until you put your hands on them. They fall apart, and you try your best to fold them back up and put them back on the shelf like the woman or the man working in the store, but you don't quite get them folded how you found them.

I got my bags, you know, like you, I got my past junk. I have condensed all my mess and put it in one place, and it's nice and neatly organized and labeled like I have OCD. You know how some of you have all the blues in one drawer, and all the reds in another drawer. All the stuff with the yellows is in this drawer. All the stuff that's green is in this drawer, socks and undies are here. You know, you folks out there that think that you got to have everything in perfect order for you to live your life. You'll have to do the same thing with your past. Organize that shit to where you can live with it and not in it.
Sometimes that may require you to go and get professional counseling or guidance from a mental health professional. Doing so is not a sign of weakness but a strength.

You are a walking, breathing, talking, living testimony, go on and create yourself as a new chapter in the book of life. You're just another one that's going to help us learn. You know, when you read the Bible, read the parables, the stories of Daniel, David, Moses, Mary, Mary Magdalene, Peter, Luke, Paul, you learned that many of these folks were jacked up. They had the sketchiest pasts but was still fit to roll with the almighty Jesus. For example, Paul was one of the most gangster of gangsters. He was one of the most conniving of conniving, but he ended up being God's blessed man. He ended up being Jesus's best man for the job of helping to save souls. Paul had plenty of baggage. His past blemishes, the not so good things of his past, is what made him the best of what he was in the present and the future.

I'm asking you to do the same because we needed Paul. Can you imagine what life would be like right now if we didn't have a Paul? What if we didn't have a Harriet Tubman, a Rosa Parks, or a Madame C.J. Walker.? You view them as great, but they were women just like you. They had their issues in their life just like you. We all have issues, and it's what you do with them that makes the difference.

So, it is my testimony that I'm not perfect. It is my testimony that I haven't been perfect. I'm gonna tell you right now, I ain't going to be perfect and I ain't trying to be perfect. I'm not trying to hide who I am, either. I'm not trying to be something that I'm not. I'm not going to disown my past. I'm not going to deny it because, as I explained, that was part of my journey in getting here, and not one of those experiences has gone in vain, and neither has yours. Yeah, there's gonna be some folks who are going to pull your shit up. They're gonna pull your credit report up. They're gonna pull your mama shitake up. They're gonna pull your daddy shitake up. They're gonna pull your spouse shitake up. Hell, they're going to pull uncles and aunties and cousins. They're going to pull mutha luvas you don't even know shitake up that happen to be associated with you and try to discredit you. They may be successful at getting other people to look at you in a different light based on that, but what you need to do is stand in who you are and that is part of you because when you stand in who you are and you stand firm and you stand strong, and you stand in your worthiness, and you are good with it can't nobody shake you. They can try. They can do their very best to throw you off your game.

It doesn't mean you won't get pissed. You're human, so standing in your shit doesn't excuse you from having feelings. It doesn't mean that you're not supposed to get upset because somebody keeps bringing up something that you did in your past when that wasn't the best time of your life. Those weren't the best decisions that you made. Don't mean you're supposed to act like the shitake ain't happen. I'm not saying that at all, but what I'm saying is when you stand and you own, and you accept, and you affirm, can't shit be taken from you because only you have the power. No one else. Don't get hung up in that. Just keep pushing. Own who you are, whose you are, and where you came from because it's all a part of the greater good, and when you do so, you do so in making me a better person. You do so in making your neighbor a better person. You do so in making those who haven't even been born yet better people. Like I said, your destiny is tied to other's destinies, so own it.

You may not even realize the different experiences in your life where you have been a servant leader, where you have been a compassionate leader, where you have displayed that you have developed the skills to be able to lead. Yes, of course, when you get into the political position that you're going for, you're going to learn even more because it's a forever learning process. It never stops. To this day, I still go to trainings. I still go to workshops. I still connect myself to people who I can learn more from.

The first thing I did when I got on the council was to request all types of information and all types of materials. It was like being in school, but I did it so I could learn the job and be the best leader that I could be for the community and the most knowledgeable person that I could be for this position, and it never stops because if it does stop, then you stop. My husband planted this blood orange tree in our backyard like two, three years ago and it hasn't grown a bit. I take that back, it just started growing just a little bit. Now I want to say it had grown maybe an inch, but it hasn't produced any fruit. I don't think you heard me. It hasn't produced any fruit because it's not receiving the nutrients or the time that it needs in order for it to blossom and produce fruit for others to enjoy, so it's the same in this political game. It's the exact same, so don't come into this thinking, oh, I can't go into this position because I've never been a leader. You have in some form or fashion, you have led, and you have led well, this is on the job training my sisters. You're not going to come to the table with it all because if you come to the table thinking you have it all again, you're gonna crash and burn. You're gonna die out. You're going to be that blood orange tree that is in my backyard that does not receive the nutrients that it needs in order to grow and blossom and feed the people. You were born to do this. You were born to lead. God created us all to be leaders, and there's a spot for all of us to lead. There's a position for all of us to lead in some kind of way. I'm asking you to take some time and really look back in your life. You may have been on a school site council, you know, when you were a kid, you might have been in student government like I was . And as I said, none of these things really came to me until I decided to run, and it was brought to my attention. I still wouldn't have thought about it. Take some time to reflect and look at your life. Look at the things that you have done to serve, to lead, to help other people. Even the fact that you picked up this book, you know, most of you are such high achievers, myself included, and high achievers tend to radiate towards other high achievers. And I know a lot of you are in your job, your current nine to five or in your own business, kicking ass and taking names you are the total badasses in your field leading projects at your job. If you're a business owner, come on now. Come on. Yeah, you may be a solopreneur, the only one working for your business, but you still leading. You're still serving. You're working with others. How many of you have stepped up and have trained or taught someone else? You have led them to being a better person. Come on now. Don't treat me and act like I'm the only one because I know I'm not and I need you to understand and know that you got to release that greatness. It's okay for you to look at yourself. Far too often, we are told that that's being self-centered, no it's self-love, and we don't do it enough. Black women, we don't do it enough colored girls, we do not do it enough, and this is the time for you to do it. It's okay. It's okay for you to sit back and look at the wonderful things that you have done for others. I will have a problem if you are sitting up here, you know, and every time you turn around, you talking about your damn self. You talking about you, you're talking about, you know, this is what I did for me. This is what I did for me.

This is what I did for me. Of course, you need to do some things for you, but it's a balance. Kendrick Lamar said it best, "Be Humble."

So, I need you to step out of your own way and recognize that you are already a leader in your own right. Yes. Now it's time for you to spread that leadership love to the masses because it's needed.

Chapter 10 - Waiting On The Perfect Storm

"Don't wait around for other people to be happy for you. Any happiness you get you've got to make yourself." – Alice Walker

Far too often, when women are approached about running for office or pursuing major leadership positions, they say that it isn't the right time or they allow someone else to tell them that it isn't their time. Regardless of what seat they're interested in pursuing, I always get this same response. It is thought that it takes, on average, a woman five to seven times to be asked to run before she considers when most of the time, men don't even have to be asked to run. Many men just run even when they ain't got no damn business running. They feel in their heart that they are the best for the job and that they are the bomb.com. They are gonna run, and they don't need anyone to give them any permission. They don't even give a damn if someone came and told them that they shouldn't run and they don't give a damn if anyone tells them they should. Many men do what the hell they want to do. But it's different for us women and especially black women. If it takes five to seven times for just women in general, can you imagine how many more times it takes for a Black woman to be asked to run before they would even consider it? Especially given that we don't see too many of us in these positions, so of course naturally it is going to be a little bit more difficult for us to even consider making that commitment.

Even when asked to consider seeking appointments, I always get women who come to me and say, I would love to serve, but I'm not, or I don't have, or not right now. They're always looking for that perfect storm, that perfect time, that perfect moment to jump in and finally go after their dreams to finally conquer the world. I can conquer the world once I get married and have children. Or when I get settled in the career that I want. Or when I have adequate finances. Or when I have, you know, this type of house or I'm driving the Porsche, or I'm wearing the Louis Vuitton. There is always a laundry list of reasons why they shouldn't move out of their current situation.

There's always this extended criterion with women and especially with the Black women who I come across. There's always these extra criteria that we put on ourselves for what that perfect time looks like. Let me tell you this, that ain't happening. There is never, ever that perfect season, or perfect time. It just doesn't exist. It's never going to happen. It never ends. If you're continuing to wait for you to decide on being that change agent or being that game player to come in and change the things in your community, your city, your state, your nation, whatever it is that you're trying to do, hell on your job if you're thinking about moving up in leadership because this is really the same thing.

But if you are waiting for that perfect moment, then you will never do it. You will never step up and run for office. You will never go after that seat on that board. You will never go for that appointment. You will never apply for a leadership position. You just won't ever do it because you always feel that there's some piece of the puzzle that's just not there. And mark my words, I'm just telling you from experience, and I know not just with myself but with other people you have seen who are successful at doing this, will tell you that there's never going to be that perfect time, just never. It just doesn't exist because perfection is not a reality and we tend to look for perfection in everything. And that's just another crutch that you're holding on to, and I'm not just talking about you. I went through the same thing too.

I talked about every reason why I shouldn't or couldn't or wasn't in regard to me running for city council than I did for the things why I should. And I found when I was looking at that list, you know, I still have that list. When I looked back years later, now that I have served, I looked and saw that I was making shit up. I was disabling myself and was creating roadblocks that didn't have to be there. You know, I created traffic on a freeway, the highway of life that didn't even exist, that didn't need to exist, and it was solely based on fear. Fear is an ugly and nasty beast. It's one of those Goliaths that you have to face in your life and not just running for public office. It's that Goliath that you have to face in life just like David faced, fought, and conquered.

Otherwise, you won't do anything except for keep saying I coulda, I woulda, I shoulda and then be stuck in a place of complacency or stuck in a place of disappointment because you didn't step out and face your fears often enough to make any significant and meaningful progress. When I go out, and I speak to women, that's what they always say, oh, I want to do it. I want to run for office, but I'm not old enough. I want to run for office, but I haven't had any children yet, and I want to run for office, but I'm not married yet, or I just got married, or I haven't been married long enough, or I've been married too long. You know, there's always all these different negative parameters that they put on themselves before they want to move forward and run for office. Then there's the experience fear they hold on to. They say, "I don't have enough experience. I haven't served in any political position. I haven't worked in politics before." Let me just share this. Let's digress a little bit before we move on. Let me just give you this bit of a golden nugget. Most of these people out here who are running for office, who are serving in office, have never done so before.

Silence.

Crickets.

That's all I hear right now - Crickets.

Most of these people who are out here running, who got elected, who are serving now, and for the most part, serving well and are successful policymakers, successful people serving in office, have never run before in their life, never had any attachments to anything political. Some weren't really fan of politics, but they were a lover of people. They cared about their community. It was more about people than politics. They weren't hung up on the position. That's what I need you to do. I need you to step away and stop looking at the nuances of all that goes into it. Yes, there are some skills that make you more successful. Yes. There are some experiences that will allow you to be more successful. Yes, there are some qualifications that you should have that make you more successful.

But oftentimes you already possess those skills and qualifications, but you just don't see it because you've gotten too hung up on titles: Congressperson, councilperson, assemblyperson, representative, state representative, board member appointees. You're so hung up on the technicalities that you have forgotten who you are and that you're worthy. You have experiences and proficiencies that you can contribute. You get so caught up, and you forget who you are because you're so busy trying to bring somebody else to the table. Oops. Oh, did I call you out? I think I just stepped on some toes there. Don't feel bad because it ain't too late because I did the same damn thing. I went in feeling that, Oh, before I do any of this I got to get my shit together, but I didn't even have a true defined path or even a definition on what the shit was that I needed to get together before I could even display and do my shit. Doing this makes us feel safe, so that's why we never ended up getting in the game and why we never ended up even being considered because we hold ourselves back waiting on that perfect moment. The perfect storm just doesn't exist. A storm is a storm.

But we will sit back and watch a dumb ass bubba run and win because a qualified woman refused to win. Then we get pissed when this pet rock starts passing ordinances and implementing policies that are detrimental to the entire town. And there they are, Sitting in position, serving for multiple terms, ,and they're dumb as rocks. A fool that doesn't have half of the experience that you have. He doesn't have half of the education that you have. His responses are so idiotic that it makes you frequently question if he even has any form of education. But this fool is being told that he is good to go, just as you are because that's the message that we put out in society, especially when it comes to white men, you are great just the way you are.

And then women we get ridiculed, chastised and downright attacked. Especially those who are mothers, you know, because I dealt with that too. You have people that will come to you and say, well, how could you serve and be a mother to your children? What? The same way that man over there is being a father to his children and serving. The same way that I can walk and chew gum. Get the hell out of here with that sexist shit. And it is usually other women who are questioning other women's ability to be a mother and work. It's important for us to show our children that we are BADASS chicks who are out here changing the world so, that they can have a better place to live, after all, what better role model do they need while raising and caring for them and keeping the household afloat.

So, we have to start to create that same way of thinking that men have. We don't need to wait. We don't need anyone else's permission. When you're running for office, the only thing that you have to wait for is the official filing period.

I'm being real with you.

I repeat: the only damn thing that you have to wait on is the filing period.

When do I submit my papers to run? That should be the only thing that you are waiting on. You don't have to wait till you get taller. You don't have to wait till you get skinnier. You don't have to wait until your hair grows to your shoulder. You don't have to wait for any of those things.

Much of what you are waiting on, you won't achieve or obtain until you get in office. You know you're going to learn, grow, develop and do some changing while you're in the position. So, if you continue to wait until you have all this shit together before you run before you step out there, it'll just never be your reality. It'll be your fantasy. It'll be like Biggie always said, "it was just a dream, I used to read Word Up magazine." That's what you'll be doing. Just dreaming while you are sitting back, reading Word Up magazine and the guy next to you who can't even touch you in terms of your greatness is going out and living your dream. The life you always wanted. And then you become upset, bitter, resentful, and sometimes hateful towards him. And sometimes, you may develop a resentment towards the world because you fought all of them, including yourself, on why you didn't step out and why you keep waiting for your shitake to be together.

You know, I have met some dynamic women who initially didn't step out, but eventually ran for office and won. You know, I met a young pregnant woman at a conference she says, this is something I truly want to do, but I was told, or they said, you know how we always had an infamous they, especially in the black community it's either "the man" or "they," who the hell are these people? Who the hell are they? And why the hell we keep listening to them because they ain't never got anything right. Not when it comes to us, they have always told us wrong. So, this young woman, she was pregnant. She was like, I'm having my first child and me and the father ain't on the up and up, but this is something I so desire. I truly desire to be on the school board. She said, but they told me that I shouldn't run because I'm not married and I have a child. And um, and I couldn't possibly relate or serve on the school board because I haven't had enough experience in having my own child. And I went on to ask her, well, what is it that you want to do? What do you want to achieve? What do you want to accomplish? What mark do you want to make in the world?

What lives do you want to change? What policies do you want to develop, what programs do you want to develop that you can accomplish and do by serving in this position that you're going after? And for her, it was school and this sister, she drilled out some of the most profound responses to my questions. I was so moved. I was so energized. I was ready to pull my checkbook out of my purse right there at that time and write her a donation check. So, I looked at her, and I said, my sister if you let one more of these damn, they' s stop you from working in your purpose, if you continue to wait for that perfect time, what more is it truly? I said, really? Think about it. What more is it that you need? Because there's a reason you feel like you should be serving in that position.

That didn't just pop up overnight, that didn't just, you know, jump up in your head. There's a reason why you want to be on the school board. There's a reason why you want to serve in this capacity because serving in public office ain't always glorious. Let me tell you that right now. So, if you're looking for a moment to where you can just become famous, just stop. I mean, it takes a lot of sacrifices to serve in public office to make changes in people's lives. It takes a lot of sacrifice on your part, and you need to be ready for that as well. But what I asked her, truly, what more is it that you need? And she couldn't come up with anything. So, I just told her this, I said look, I see someone standing in front of me who knows what they want. Who feels they have what they need in order to do what it is they want? The only thing I don't see is you moving forward and getting what you want.

I mean, your finances will never be perfect. Your marriage will never be perfect. Your parenthood will never be perfect, your job will never be perfect. Your car, your house, I mean the streets you live on, none of that will ever be perfect. You will never be perfect. So if that's what's holding you back, I ask you today while you are reading these words, give yourself permission to be imperfect, so be that imperfect person and move forward and live your dream, to be imperfect, to take your imperfect self, your imperfect conditions, your imperfect surroundings, your imperfect family. Your imperfect bank accounts and step forward and take on that challenge because there's never a good time. Never. The stars never quite fully line up.

Will you sometimes have to give up some things? Yes! You may have to give up that job that you've been at for 10, 15 years to do what it is that you love, but why should that matter if you are giving it up to do what it is that you love.

You are running.

You want to run for public office because that's something that you love. I'm not telling you tomorrow to go and hand in your resignation to your job unless truly that is what you need to do in order for you to be free.

Come on now. Come on. I'm just being real. We said, in the beginning, we were going to be real with each other, and I told you I wasn't going to give you no "fluff and bull" as my grandma, and good friend Valtina would frequently say because I don't do that. Right now, you're being held captive. You know you were a slave in your own life because of other people's negative chatter or your own self-defeating thoughts. Stop holding yourself back because you are waiting on still waters. The water will never be calm enough. The clouds will never be light enough. The sky will never be clear enough. It just won't. The wind will not be as gracious as you want, ever. You've got to get out there and weather the storm just as it is because if this is truly for you, if this is truly your purpose if serving people is truly for you, then you will be fully equipped. You will have all of the gear that you need in order to weather the storm. And if you don't have it right now, some kind of way you will end up getting it because that's just how it works. That's how God is.

If you are into the laws of attraction, you believe that your thoughts can allow you to manifest your destiny. The key is that you have to truly believe. I will say this is the one thing that you can't go in half-ass with. You could half-ass a lot of stuff and get away with it, we all know we do it at our jobs. We half-ass a report and only give 70% when we could've given 110 percent. We only gave them 70 percent because the folks we work for keep getting on our nerves, then we half-ass things with our kids, our family, our spouses.
Come on now, please don't act like I'm making up something.
The only thing I'm going to say is you that you CANNOT half-ass on yourself. You've done it. You've tried it. That's why you're frustrated. That's why you haven't pushed and accomplished and gotten where you feel you need to be. That's why you haven't moved on to the next goal, and that includes those of you who are in public office right now. You ran, you have won and served your office successfully, but you are stuck.

You haven't gone to the next level because you've been half-assing yourself. You give more to other people. You'll give 90, 80, 100, 110 percent to everybody else and only give yourself 20. Stop only giving yourself 20 percent. Hell, some of y'all only 2 percenting yourselves.

Is that fair?

I'm not trying to put any pressure on you, but I'm putting pressure on because you decided that you're too afraid that you care more about what others think about you than you think about yourself. You're too anal, you're too OCD, whatever you want to call it, and waiting for perfection when God has already told you perfection doesn't exist. Come on now. I just dropped that little nugget on you. You ain't perfect. Nothing is perfect. Nothing on this planet is perfect. The only perfect person is God. Because you are waiting on perfection, you are waiting for something that will never happen. I'm not perfect you hear that I admit I'm not perfect, but because you are waiting on that perfect moment, somebody else can't live in that purpose. It's a trickle effect. It's like, what's that movie that I was always scared of that my kid and my husband are always trying to have me watch, that movie Final Destination. You know how that movie is, focusing on a chain reaction of deaths, so we see multiple people dying from horrific events that are all interconnected to one another. You know a woman is drinking lemonade while driving and then spills lemonade on her lap, which causes her to swerve into the next lane, which causes the man in the car next to her to slam on his brakes. His slamming on the brakes causes the truck driver behind him to slam on his brakes. And when he slams on his brakes, it causes his truck to swerve. And then it causes the rope holding the logs together to break. And then that causes the logs to fall and tumble across the freeway, which causes the other cars to stop. And then there's one stopped car because they weren't paying attention, to hit the logs, and when they hit the logs, they cause this car to explode. You get it. You understand what the hell I'm talking about.

That's how it is with your life on what you choose to do and what you choose not to do. You are affecting other people's lives.

Like anything, there will be a need to get your shitake together and prepare. You may need to get some training, consulting and guidance, or volunteer on someone else's campaign to get you going and started in the right direction. The key here is getting going. But don't use that as an excuse to overthink shit. You know how we do it, we'll be in training mode forever, hiding behind fear, but saying its preparation — or we'll run around doing a bunch of busy work bamboozling ourselves into thinking that we are really getting something accomplished.

Get the hell out of here with that.

Just the simple fact that you decided to purchase and read this book tells me that there is a part of you that is ready. You're ready to serve. You're ready to be that catalyst of your community. So, the time is now. Don't wait any longer because we need you.

Chapter 11 - Who Gone Check Me Boo?

I am deliberate and afraid of nothing. – Audre Lorde

Hunty child! Now you know how I see us Black women, even when the world we live in doesn't frequently depict us in such a positive light. I sat on this book, had it brewing inside of me for many years. Not moving forward or doing anything to make my vision, mission, goal, and dream of being a vessel and resource for Black women in politics a reality. Initially, I worried about the backlash that I would receive or the many who just wouldn't or didn't want to understand this important message. Sadly, when I made the announcement that I would be writing this book to my good friends, one of them cautioned me not to write this text.

My girl said, "Aren't you afraid of being blackballed out of the game?" And she told me that I should take heed to what could happen if I write a word that could potentially exclude the most dominant players in politics: Men, (in particular white men) and white women. I was like gurl, have you taken a good look around you? We have already been blackballed out of the game of politics. See, my girlfriend fell into the trap that some of the insecure Black women tend to fall into, and that is making it comfortable for everyone else but themselves. It was my husband that said, "who gives a S.H.I.T.! You have a message inside of you that so many Black women need and have been waiting to hear, so get ta' writing." I just envisioned an image of Martin Lawrence when he would say, "get ta' steppin!" on the Martin show. Okay, okay, okay, I just had one of my ADD soapbox moments, which happens often, but with a lesson for you too; Conquer your fears and procrastination, because someone's destiny depends on it.

Many Black women consider politics but are often dissuaded because of the true reality of their perceptions of not being accepted in a field that over centuries has proven to not be a very friendly one to us Black folks and especially Black women. Even back in the 1950s, Chisholm realized this. She was frequently encouraged to consider a political career, but she frequently felt that she faced a "double handicap" as being both Black and female[x]. As a Black woman that faced a time when I was asked to consider running for public office, I felt the same way. For quite some time, it was this same bull-shitake way of thinking that delayed me in taking the leap forward. It took some major soul searching and realizing the fact that I was just as good (if not better) as any other person serving or running, in order for me to go ahead and answer my calling. So glad I did, because I ran, won, and was one of the most successful at serving the people of my city.

It was back in 2012 when I decided to take a stab at representing and serving in the public sector. During the period of my political self-discovery and preparation to run for public office, I searched high and low for books like this one. Unfortunately, they didn't exist. I looked for a read that would be straight forward and honest about what I could and ultimately would end up experiencing as a black woman running for office in a field that is predominately pale, male, and stale (No, I didn't stutter. Yes, you read correctly). A book that would give me some insight on not only what it is like running, serving, and having a general interest in public office, but what that would look like as a woman who is Black. Many of the books out there either focus on the history of white women in politics or only provide you with the steps in running a campaign. Most of these books are written by and from the perspective of white men and women. It is my hope that this book succeeds in aiming at filling those gaps. Throughout my doctoral program, it was constantly drilled into my head that a change agent must seek to make the world a better place by filling in the gaps. This S.H.I.T. is my attempt to do just that.

Another reason why I felt that it was so ever important to write this book was the fact that there aren't any others like it out there. There just aren't. Outside of minimal research conducted by organizations that are Black women-centered, there isn't much literature out there regarding the subject matter. Now, don't get me wrong. There isn't much out there about women and politics period! When Secretary of State Hillary Clinton decided to throw her hat in the ring for President, it was at that time when various champions of women's rights began to focus literature on women in politics. That was great! The dilemma of women of color not seeping through those pages still existed. Don't get me wrong, Hillary Clinton is a notable force in the women's movement. She stepped up and took on the challenge of running for a presidency that was not in her favor and against many odds. So, I clearly understand why all the "I'm every woman" books wanted to focus on Secretary Clinton. But, many of these texts skimmed over the fact that Hillary Clinton wasn't the first to charter the shark-infested waters. There were several before her. One of the most prolific Presidential candidates of all times was Shirley Chisholm, a Black woman who was "unbought and unbossed." "Fighting Shirley" was the first black woman to break ground into Congress and to seek the political party's nomination for president of the United States (Michals, 2015). [xi]As a Black woman running in the 1970s, she was hit with a great deal of push back. Chisholm was blocked from participating in televised primary debates, and after taking legal action, was permitted to make just one speech. Still, students, women, and minorities followed the "Chisholm Trail." She entered 12 primaries and garnered 152 of the delegates' votes (10% of the total)—despite an under-financed campaign and contentiousness from the predominantly male Congressional Black Caucus. Michals, Debra. "Shirley Chisholm." National Women's History Museum. (Michals, 2015)[xii]

We have been doing the damn thang in our communities, as well as other folks' communities from the beginning of time. We have proven to be successful thought leaders, taking the business world by storm, and are leading in the efforts in higher education degrees obtained. We have been the mothers of this nation, lending our milk (literally) in an effort to provide nourishment for all. Black women, it is time for us to wean this grown baby. The political oppressors will need to release their vice grip on our tits because we have served as the wet nurse breastfeeding them for far too long and we are drying up like the hot ass desert[xiii].

Now you didn't think that we were going to spend all of this productive time together for me to send you off feeling self-defeated, deflated, and in a Kumbaya moment. Now is the time where I give you the meat and potatoes - the call to action and the steps to help get you over the hump and making the bold step to run.

- Get Up and Run – It is as simple as the words coming out of your mouth. You can't win if you don't run. My dad always says that to me about playing the lottery, so it seemed like a good idea to share this ancient wisdom with you. You don't have to have prior political or campaign experience. Just get up and do it. The burning desire will not go away, because it is your calling. As a matter of fact, it is going to increase day by day. You will soon start to think that your mind, your house, your car, and all of your surroundings are bugged because you will start to see that just about everything that is presented to you will be encouraging you to run. You will begin to dream about you running, winning, and serving.

- Start Researching – Don't wait until the last darn minute. Many, actually, most of the women that I work within my political coaching and consulting practice wait until the 9th hour before they decide to run for public office. It is possible to do this and win, but not the best route to victory. Start building out your plan 1- 2 years before running. Research the position that you are interested in, learn everything about the person currently holding the position and their campaign efforts. Interview other dynamic Black women serving office or any elected that you are impressed with. Ask them to mentor you. Don't be afraid to ask them to mentor you. They will either say yes or no. Start telling people who care about you that you want to run for public office because this makes you accountable. Start building your BADASS team of people that will support you during your campaign the moment you start telling folks you are running. Again, don't wait until the last darn minute.

- Recruit Another Good Black Woman – Ok, I couldn't talk you into running. No problem! Not everyone will run. We need BADASS women to serve in other capacities. So, if you will not run, recruit another fierce Black woman to run. When you ask her to run, then support her emotionally and financially.

- Personally, Donate and Raise Money Before, During, and After the Campaign- No amount is too small. If you only have $5 a month to give, GIVE IT! Those small-dollar donations add up. Some of the most successful campaigns have been those with grassroots small-dollar donations that have added up to millions. Host house parties and fundraisers for Black women candidates. Send donations to Black women that you don't even know, but support their vision and platform. I do it all the time.

- Stop Giving Money to Organizations That Do Not Support Black Women Candidates and Politicians – This is straight and to the point. Stop giving your hard-earned dollars to entities that don't want to work hard on behalf of supporting Black women in politics. I can't get any clearer than this. This includes political parties on the national, state, and local levels.

- Work on A Campaign – Working on a campaign is the best steps in preparing to run yourself, or helping another candidate out. I probably wouldn't have ever run for office if it hadn't been for me first volunteering years ago on Kamala Harris' campaign. I gained so many golden nuggets from that experience. Volunteer experience can also lead to paid campaign positions. We need more Black women running campaigns, being political consultants, you name it there aren't enough of us out there doing it. I haven't met one political operative that didn't get their start in politics by not volunteering and/or working on a campaign.

- If You're Not Willing to Run, Work for An Elected, or a Government Agency – You may be saying I read through this entire book, but I still ain't running. Ok fine. I know when to choose my battles. Black women need to also consider working for a politician or in government. I can't tell you how few Black women are leading within governmental entities. I haven't seen very many Black women that are city managers. So, we need you on all fronts of politics.

- Pray, Pray, Pray, and Then Pray Some Mo – Not one person or group can kill what God has called for you. Pray like you have never prayed before. Pray that you are able to discern the steps that you need to take and the serpents that you will need to cut or avoid. Pray in the morning, afternoon, and night for wholeness.

- Don't Trip If They Sleep on You – If you don't get the support, endorsement, or blessings of organizations, committees, caucuses, clubs, etc., no worries, keep pushing on. You don't need it to get to where you are going. It helps but is not required. Let them sleep on you. The same folks that count you out tend to be the same folks that will have to congratulate you.

- Get Your Armor Ready – The unfortunate fact is that your journey to get that political seat may be a heavy and treacherous battle. No problem! No worries! You are part of the BADASS crew, so just get your BADASS prepared for the battle. Get your weapons of mass destruction together, so that you are prepared to destroy anyone or anything that is deviously trying to stop this movement.

- Be Willing to Ask for Help – This isn't a movement in a silo. You cannot and should not do this alone. Swallow your pride, kick your fear in the ass, tell complacency were to go, and step out of your zone of discomfort, and get the help that you need so that you can become that Political BADASS ™.

- Don't Be Afraid or Too Polite To Call The Bull shit What it is - Bullshit – This is a time where you will have to call a spade a spade and treat them as such. If you come head to head with racist, sexist, misogynistic behaviors and actions from others, call that shit out. We often tip toeing around this offensive bull shit because we are trying to be "politically correct." Frack That! The political correctness has done nothing but allowed us to be in modern-day bondage aka SLAVERY. It does not work in favor of Black women. Congresswoman Maxine Waters said it best "We have been shut down, because others have defined us. When they said to us about 10 – 15 years ago, she's playing the race card, you should say yes, I am, and I got a lot more I'm gonna play. We stop calling a racist a racist because they said that's all you do. You don't do anything else. Don't let these people intimidate or scare you. You got to get in the fight. It's time to take off the handcuffs. It's time to get in it and call it like it is." [xiv]So, even Auntie Maxine has given you permission to say what needs to be said, many people will appreciate you for it.

- Be Willing To Face Generational Patterns and Kick Them To The Curb – So what your momma was on crack, your dad is incarcerated, you were a teenage mother, everyone in your family battled alcoholism, you are the only one in your family or circle with a college degree, this list can go on and on. The bottom line is none of that defines you. So, stop letting it hold you back.

- Be Willing to Be A Student – Allow yourself to be schooled. Be willing to be a sponge and learn as much as you can learn. If you know it all, if you have all the answers, then you will stay where you are. Even the greatest of all times have had to reach out and get some help and support. Get a mentor, a coach, a confidant that will be willing to give you the real deal and not the fluff and bull. Someone that is going to bring the best you out and to the table.

- Focus on Being You and Not A Part of Any Establishment – Stop playing small where you blend into the group(s) that you are a part of. Don't be afraid to be a shining star and lead from the front. Don't feel a need to "Be like Mike." Do you, Boo! Although, you could and should be connected to organizations, political parties, coalitions, remember that you are an asset to them a unique piece to their puzzle. It should be you that draws the voters to vote for you. You may get their attention by who you are affiliated with, but it should be the authentic you that gets them to the polls.

- Don't Let Them Make You Commit A Black on Black Crime – There will be those that will let all hell break loose before seeing the comradery of Black women. There will be those that will do all they can to keep you and other Black women from coming together in harmony and peace because they know that one Black woman is a force, but when multiple Black women work together, that creates a synergistic BADASSery that is very tough to break. The evil dwellers trying to disrupt this harmony will be White men and women, Latino men and women, Asian/Pacific Islander men and women, and even Black men and women. I remember when I ran for office, there were so many naysayers and evil dwellers that made every attempt to keep me from developing a cordial relationship with the only other Black woman that served on the council in which I was to serve. They told me all types of evil untruths about her, and I am sure they did the same to her regarding me. Well, we defied the opposition and became friends. She ended up being the most solid confidant that I had on the council. So, when they come to you trying to disrupt Black women harmony, give them the middle finger and show them the door. Get to know your sisters for yourself and make the choice on the type of relationships that you will have.

- When You Win Bring It – When you win your race, hold to your word. Don't make big grandiose promises that you cannot keep. Continue to work with and connect with your constituents. Remember, they were the ones that voted you in and will have to be the ones that will vote you back in should you run again. Don't just show up when it's campaign season. Be accountable, accessible, and transparent. That is the foolproof plan of being a successful politician.

- Be Unapologetically Black and a Woman, because it is normal to do so – Always be bold and standing in who you truly are. If you start off faking the funk, should you run and win, you will spend your entire time serving as a FAKE. Just like those swap meet and beauty shop handbags, we spoke of earlier. If you speak with an accent- ROCK-IT!. If you engage in Ebonics every now and then – ROCK-IT! If you wear cornrows, locs, or a natural afro – ROCK-IT! If you have SWAG that others can't understand – ROCK-IT! There is nothing wrong with the real you. Those that attempt to place you in a box of what a politician should look, talk, walk, or be are the ones that require correcting. Don't be afraid to be unbossed and unbought. You don't have to explain why your light is so bright, like the lighthouse illuminating a town. Trying to make you something that you are not is not normal. Nor should you be trying to make it the new normal. Black women, you are the precious jewels of the earth. One of my favorite quotes is by Iyanla Vanzant, "Be careful not to normalize the dysfunction."

- If You Lose – I'm not going to spend a lot of time on this one. Dust yourself off, count it as a lesson, and get up and run again. Pretty damn simple.

My sisters, this is just a shortlist of positive, actionable items that can be done to improve things for us. We don't have to sit and wait while the political parties decide whether they want to be our friend or our foe. We don't need to sit around in desperation like a young teen sitting home alone on prom night, only to realize her date ain't coming through. We hold the power! As we have clearly demonstrated in the 2018 and years past elections. We don't have another second to waste, because our children, our spouses, our education, our businesses, and our lives depend on us taking charge and making a change.[xv]

The bottom line is Black Women Get Things Done! So, get to it! Tom Perez, Current Chair of The Democratic Party, said it best "Black women are the backbone of the Democratic party." [xvi]We are also beginning to witness Black women bringing up the rear of the Republican party too. If you want to be a sideline madame, complaining, and pushing everyone else out there to step up and do something, I ain't talking to you. If you want to remain a keyboard gangsta that will only use your voice to argue, cuss out, and develop ineffective policies via social media platforms, I ain't talking to you.

Just remember that they told Shirley Chisolm that she was "TOO." She was told that she was too radical (me too), too Black (me too), and too anti-establishment (me too). Sidebar convo: Hot damn! I think we have just created a new hashtag movement, #MeTooToo . Chisolm's perfect response to her naysayers was, "If you can't support me, if you can't endorse me, get out of my way." [xvii]

Before we part ways, here is the last bit of advice that I want to give you, which is so profound, and you will need to read these statements daily and commit them to memory:

BE BOLD! BE RADICAL! BE A DISRUPTOR! YOU GOT THIS, SO GO OUT THERE AND WIN!

It has been my ultimate desire that the contents of this book were as fruitful to you as they have been to me. It is my hope that I provided you with the love (I know it was tough) and guidance that you need in order for you to make that decision to lead, whether or not that includes you running for public office. I have dedicated my life to preaching (yes, this is my ministry as unorthodox as it may appear) this message around the world, so that more women, women of color, and especially black women take the necessary actions to step up and take on leadership positions. I urge you to go and check out my website www.thepoliticalbadass.com, all my social media platforms, as I provide a host of free resources and useful information.

I have also taken the time to create Becoming a Political BADASS™, a new and dynamic mentor, coaching, and training program designed for women to get all of the information, tools, resources, and support in order to run BADASS political campaigns and be successful leaders once they get in office.

LET'S DO THIS TOGETHER!

About the Author

Tonya Burke is a sought-after expert, speaker, coach, political consultant and strategist, author of On The Edge of Greatness: A Real Conversation on How Black Women Can Take Over By Powerfully Running For Office, and Bestselling Co-Author of God Doesn't Want You To Be Broke; An award-winning politician (retired) and community leader that has been advocating as early as elementary school.

Tonya is the Founder and CEO of Hidden Gems Enterprise, a boutique political coaching, and government relations consulting firm.

Most commonly known as The Political Badass ™, as she Educates, Empowers, and Engages women to run for political office; seek leadership positions in the public and private sectors; and help leaders of leaders use their inner superhero powers, gifts, and purpose, to make their mark in the world.

Tonya has been featured in a number of publications, including: The Atlantic, Black Voice News, Press Enterprise, Precinct Reporter, Los Angeles Sentinel, Black Girls Guide to Politics, Noteworthy, and Blavity. She has appeared as a panel expert with former Secretary of State and Senator Hillary Clinton and Congresswoman Maxine Waters. Tonya is a reappearing commentator on Canadian Television (CTV),

Tonya received her B.A. in Psychology from the University of California, Santa Cruz; her M.A. in Clinical Psychology from Pepperdine University.
Tonya resides in Perris, California. She enjoys spending time with her husband Jason and three children Devon, Brianna, and Jaylyn.

Stay Connected

Facebook: https://www.facebook.com/ThePoliticalBadass/
Instagram: https://www.instagram/politicalgem/
LinkedIn: https://www.linkedin.com/in/hidden-gems-enterprise
Twitter: https://twitter.com/PoliticalGems
YouTube Channel: *The Political Badass*

[i] Michals, D. (2015). *Shirley Chisholm*. Retrieved from National Women's History Museum. 2015. https://www.womenshistory.org/education-resources/biographies/shirley-chisholm

[ii] Lockhart, P. (2018). *In 2018, Black women like Ayanna Pressley are fighting for political power - and winning*. Retrieved from https://www.vox.com/policy-and-politics/2018/9/5/17823582/ayanna-pressley-massachusetts-black-women-voters-2018-midterm-elections

[iii] Waters, M. (2017). *Congressional Black Caucus Town Hall on Civil Rights*. Retrieved from https://www.c-span.org/video/?434372-1/congressional-black-caucus-holds-town-hall-civil-rights

[iv] Merriam-Webster Dictionary (2019). *Naysayer Definition*. Retrieved from https://www.merriam-webster.com/dictionary/naysayer

[v] Wier, K. (2013). *Feel like a fraud? You're not alone. Many graduate students question whether they are prepared to do the work they do. Here's how to overcome that feeling and recognize your strengths*. Retrieved from https://www.apa.org/gradpsych/2013/11/fraud (p. 24)

[vi] Towns Chart. (2018). *City of Perris Education Demographics*. Retrieved from https://www.towncharts.com/California/Education/Perris-city-CA-Education-data.html

[vii] Black Women In Politics (2018). *Black Women Candidates Running for Office*. Retrieved from: http://database.blackwomeninpolitics.com/

[viii] Black Women In Politics (2018). *Black Women Candidates Running for Office*. Retrieved from: http://database.blackwomeninpolitics.com/

[ix] Badu, E., Young, A. (2000). *Bag Lady. Album: Mama's Got A Gun*. Motown Records.

[x] Michals, D. (2015). *Shirley Chisholm*. Retrieved from National Women's History Museum. 2015. https://www.womenshistory.org/education-resources/biographies/shirley-chisholm

[xi] Michals, D. (2015). *Shirley Chisholm*. Retrieved from National Women's History Museum. 2015. https://www.womenshistory.org/education-resources/biographies/shirley-chisholm

[xii] Michals, D. (2015). *Shirley Chisholm*. Retrieved from National Women's History Museum. 2015. https://www.womenshistory.org/education-resources/biographies/shirley-chisholm

[xiii] Burke, T. (2019) *The Democratic Party Doesn't Care Enough About Black Women, So Sis, Save Yourself* - Blavity. (n.d.). Retrieved from https://blavity.com/the-democratic-party-doesnt-care-enough-about-black-women-so-sis-save-yourself

[xiv] Waters, M. (2017). *Congressional Black Caucus Town Hall on Civil Rights*. Retrieved from https://www.c-span.org/video/?434372-1/congressional-black-caucus-holds-town-hall-civil-rights

[xv] Burke, T. (2019) *The Democratic Party Doesn't Care Enough About Black Women, So Sis, Save Yourself* - Blavity. (n.d.). Retrieved from https://blavity.com/the-democratic-party-doesnt-care-enough-about-black-women-so-sis-save-yourself

[xvi] Black Women In Politics (2018). *Black Women Candidates Running for Office*. Retrieved from: http://database.blackwomeninpolitics.com/

[xvii] Wier, K. (2013). *Feel like a fraud? You're not alone. Many graduate students question whether they are prepared to do the work they do. Here's how to overcome that feeling and recognize your strengths*. Retrieved from https://www.apa.org/gradpsych/2013/11/fraud (p. 24)

Made in the USA
Lexington, KY
14 December 2019